C000126403

Buonissimo!

RYLAND
PETERS
& SMALL
LONDON NEW YORK

Buonissimo!

easy modern recipes for traditional Italian cooking

Silvana Franco   Ursula Ferrigno   Clare Ferguson   Elsa Petersen-Schepelern

Senior Designer Susan Downing
Commissioning Editor Elsa Petersen-Schepelern
Editor Kathy Steer
Production Tamsin Curwood
Art Director Gabriella Le Grazie
Publishing Director Alison Starling
Indexer Hilary Bird

Published in the United Kingdom in 2002
by Ryland Peters & Small
Kirkman House,
12–14 Whitfield Street
London W1T 2RP
www.rylandpeters.com
10 9 8 7 6 5 4 3 2 1

ISBN 1 84172 334 7

A catalogue record for this book is available from the
British Library

Printed and bound in China

Notes
All spoon measurements are level.

All eggs are large, unless otherwise specified.
Uncooked or partly cooked eggs should not be
served to the very young, the very old, those with
compromised immune systems, or to pregnant women.

To sterilize preserving jars, wash the jars in hot,
soapy water and rinse in boiling water. Put in a large
saucepan and add water to cover. With the lid on,
bring the water to the boil and continue boiling for
15 minutes. Turn off the heat, then leave the jars in the
hot water until just before they are to be filled. Invert
the jars onto clean kitchen towels to dry. Sterilize the
lids for 5 minutes by boiling. Jars should be filled and
sealed while still hot.

Recipes in this book have previously been published in
other Ryland Peters & Small books (see page 144).

contents

Buonissimo ...

Italian is everyone's favourite food – even if you can't boil an egg, it's a good bet that you can cook pasta, stir in a sauce, toss a salad and pour a glass of wine. So that's Italian – you know you love it, and you can make it.

Buonissimo builds on those skills you didn't know you had – with easy, modern versions of Italy's great traditional recipes. Cook your own pizza – from scratch. Make delicious antipasti to serve before the meal. Prepare fish, meat and poultry in the simple, easy flavourful way Italians do. Serve them with Italian vegetables – then follow up with those splendid puddings for which Italy is so famous. Cook Italian for family meals, casual lunches or elegant dinner parties: *Buonissimo!* will show you how.

Buonissimo means the 'absolute best' in Italian, and the recipes you'll find in this book are some of the best Italian dishes, certainly they are some of our favourites. However, they're just a selection. Try them, and see how easy it is – we hope they'll give you confidence and encourage you to try more Italian cooking.

antipasti

These simple savoury biscuits are delicious with anchovy, but you can try other variations, such as sun-dried tomato pesto or a pinch of crushed chillies.

anchovy
pinwheels

50 g canned anchovy fillets, finely chopped

500 g puff pastry, ready-to-roll or frozen and thawed

plain flour, for dusting

1 egg, beaten

2 non-stick baking sheets, brushed with water

Makes about 60

Using a mortar and pestle or small bowl and the back of a spoon, mash the anchovies with 1 teaspoon water to form a paste. Keep adding water until a smooth, brushable liquid results.

Put the pastry onto a lightly floured work surface and roll out to a rectangle about 5 mm thick.

Using a pastry brush, brush the anchovy mixture all over the surface (not too thick, or the taste will be too strong), then brush the far edge with beaten egg. Starting at the edge nearest you, roll up the pastry into a sausage shape about 3 cm thick and press the egg-washed edge to seal. Chill in the refrigerator for 30 minutes.

Using a sharp knife, cut the sausage crossways into 5 mm slices and arrange apart on the baking sheets.

Bake, in batches if necessary, in a preheated oven at 200°C (400°F) Gas 6 for about 10–12 minutes until crisp and golden. Remove from the oven, let cool for about 3 minutes, then transfer to a wire rack to cool completely. Serve immediately or store in an airtight container for up to 3 days.

Homemade cheese straws taste much better than the bought variety, and are very easy to make.

spice-speckled
cheese straws

150 g plain flour, plus extra for dusting

½ teaspoon salt

1 teaspoon dry mustard

50 g Cheddar cheese, grated

2 tablespoons freshly grated Parmesan cheese

60 g unsalted butter, chilled and cut into small pieces

1 egg yolk

juice of ½ lemon

paprika, for dusting (optional)

2 baking sheets, greased

Makes 36

Put the flour, salt, mustard and cheeses into a food processor and pulse to mix. Add the butter and pulse until the mixture resembles fine breadcrumbs.

Mix the egg yolk and lemon juice in a small jug, then pour into the processor with the motor running. Stop mixing when the mixture forms a dough. Transfer to a lightly floured surface and knead briefly to form a ball.

Roll out the dough to a rectangle 5 mm thick. Using a hot, sharp knife, cut into strips 1 x 7 cm. Twist into spirals and arrange well apart on the baking sheets.

Bake in a preheated oven at 180°C (350°F) Gas 4 for 10 minutes until golden. Remove from the oven, dust with paprika, if using, then let cool on the baking sheets. Serve immediately or store in an airtight container for up to 3 days.

Crostini and bruschetta are the easiest, most delicious of all antipasti – just good bread, toasted, then topped with whatever you please. Make big ones (bruschette) for lunch, or lots of little ones (crostini) as bite-sized party foods.

crostini and bruschetta

Crostini

1 baguette

your choice of toppings from the list below

Bruschetta

Italian bread of your choice, such as ciabatta, focaccia, puglièse or crusty country bread

1–2 garlic cloves, halved

a large baking sheet

Makes about 30 crostini

To make crostini, cut a baguette into 1 cm slices and arrange on a baking sheet. Bake in a preheated oven at 200°C (400°F) Gas 6 until lightly golden, about 3–4 minutes. Don't let them become too crisp or they will break when people take a bite.

Remove from the oven and let cool on a wire rack. They can be kept in an airtight container for up to 1 week. When ready to serve, crisp them again in a preheated oven at 200°C (400°F) Gas 6 for a few minutes. Remove from the heat, then add your choice of toppings – if using cheese you want to melt, put it on top before returning to the oven.

To make bruschetta, cut thick slices of bread, then rub with a cut garlic clove. Put the slices into a stove-top grill pan or under a preheated grill and cook until golden brown. Alternatively, cook over a medium-hot barbecue until golden brown.

Toppings Choose no more than 2–3 toppings or the flavours will be too confused and, if making bite-sized crostini, the toppings will fall off. Choose from the pizza toppings on page 15, or other choices include:

• Finely sliced Parma ham

• Parmesan shavings

• Caperberries or capers

• Cherry tomatoes, halved

• Oven-dried tomatoes with Fontina cheese

• Flaked char-grilled tuna with spring onions

• Fontina cheese, pancetta strips and cracked black pepper

• Smoked or poached salmon

• Char-grilled peppers or aubergine

• Anchovies with melted mozzarella.

Mini versions of Italian pizza are perfect for partying. Use half-cooked pizza bases from an Italian delicatessen, and cut out mini rounds with a biscuit cutter. The same deli can provide a selection of delicious ready-made toppings, and you can also make others.

mini pizzas

4 Italian pizza bases, about 25 cm diameter

olive oil, for brushing

your choice of toppings from the list below

4 cm biscuit cutter

several non-stick baking sheets

Makes 28

Using the biscuit cutter, cut out rounds from the pizza bases, then arrange on several baking sheets spaced well apart. Brush with olive oil and add your choice of toppings. Bake in a preheated oven at 200°C (400°F) Gas 6 for about 5 minutes or until piping hot.

If using cheese toppings, brush the pizza bases with olive oil and bake in a preheated oven at 200°C (400°F) Gas 6 for about 3 minutes first, then add cheese toppings of your choice and heat through for 1–2 minutes until softly melted, but not running away.

Variation

Instead of store-bought pizza bases, you can use slices of bread, toasted, then cut out with a biscuit cutter.

Pizza toppings Don't use more than 3–4 ingredients on each pizza or the flavours will be too complicated:

• Red pesto brushed over the surface, then topped with a curl of char-grilled yellow pepper and half an oven-dried garlic-spiked tomato (page 116), then sprinkled with fresh thyme leaves

• Fontina cheese with anchovy and a dot of red pesto

• Char-grilled yellow pepper with roasted baby artichokes

• Mozzarella, anchovy and dried oregano

• Sautéed mushrooms with Gruyère, Gorgonzola and mozzarella.

Bagna cauda means 'hot bath', and this dip from Piedmont in north-west Italy is mellow, smooth and intensely flavourful. The crisp, sweet, mild vegetables offset the salty flavour of the sauce.

bagna cauda

125 g unsalted butter

6–8 garlic cloves, crushed to a purée

90 ml extra virgin olive oil

100 g canned anchovy fillets, drained, chopped and mashed

Your choice of:

red, yellow or orange peppers (but not green), cut into 8 wedges and deseeded

white wax peppers, halved and deseeded

celery stalks

chicory (Belgian endive)

trevise (radicchio)

inner leaves from cos lettuce

spring onions

baby asparagus

cauliflower florets

broccoli florets, quartered lengthways

fennel bulbs, cut into wedges lengthways

sprigs of flat leaf parsley

Serves 4–8

Put the butter and garlic into a non-stick frying pan and heat gently until the butter has melted. Transfer to a blender and add the olive oil and anchovies. Purée for 2–3 minutes, then transfer to a serving bowl. The bowl of dip should be kept hot over a low candle flame.

Surround the hot dip with the prepared vegetables and serve.

Note The traditional method is to put the butter and puréed garlic into a shallow terracotta dish and stir for 5–10 minutes over low to medium heat. Add the anchovy fillets and mash over the heat. Add the oil, reheat gently, then serve as in main recipe.

Vegetables are delicious grilled – the charred bits have a delightfully smoky flavour. Use typical Mediterranean vegetables, bursting with ripeness and colour.

grilled vegetables

4 medium yellow courgettes

4 medium green courgettes

4 long narrow aubergines or 8 small Japanese aubergines

2 long red peppers, halved and deseeded, stems intact if possible

2 long yellow or orange peppers, halved and deseeded, stems intact if possible

2 large, mild red chillies, halved and deseeded (optional)

olive oil, for coating

sea salt and freshly ground black pepper

Marinade

500 ml extra virgin olive oil

sea salt and whole black peppercorns, crushed

4 sprigs of fresh thyme or oregano, coarsely chopped

125 ml white wine vinegar

a stove-top grill pan

Serves 8

To prepare the vegetables, cut the courgettes lengthways into 5 mm slices and cut the aubergines lengthways into 1 cm slices. Put the pepper halves, chillies, if using, courgettes and aubergines into separate plastic bags. Add some olive oil, salt and pepper to each bag and shake to coat the vegetables with oil.

Heat a stove-top grill pan over medium heat until hot. Add the peppers skin side down, put a heavy weight such as a saucepan on top and cook until dark and charred with marks. Turn the peppers over, put the saucepan back on top and cook until tender. If you want to remove the skins, put the peppers into a small saucepan and cover with a lid – the skins will steam off and you won't lose any of the delicious juices. Put the chillies, if using, onto the preheated stove-top grill pan and cook for about 2 minutes on each side until dark and charred with marks. Using a sharp knife, slice the chillies lengthways into fine strips.

Working in batches, put the courgettes and aubergines onto the grill pan and cook until tender and charred with marks – the courgettes will take about 2 minutes on each side, the aubergines about 2–3 minutes on each side, or until cooked all the way through. Put all the vegetables into separate containers.

To make the marinade, put the olive oil, salt, pepper and thyme or oregano into a small saucepan and heat, stirring constantly. Remove from the heat and carefully add the vinegar (take care or the oil may spatter). Pour over the vegetables. Let marinate for at least 30 minutes, then serve.

Alternatively, the vegetables may be packed into sterilized jars (see page 4), covered with the olive oil mixture and refrigerated. When ready to serve, let return to room temperature first.

Peppers are ideal ingredients in antipasti: they respond well to grilling and roasting, two methods that develop the natural sugars. Mixed with salty anchovies and sharp pickled caperberries or capers, they really come into their own. This recipe is from southern Italy – easy, elegant and delicious.

peperoni farciti

4 red or yellow peppers, quartered lengthways and deseeded

16 canned anchovy fillets, rinsed and drained

16 caperberries or 2 tablespoons capers, rinsed and drained

a small bunch of fresh marjoram or oregano, chopped

2 tablespoons extra virgin olive oil

freshly ground black pepper

Serves 4

Arrange the pepper wedges in a large roasting dish or tin.

Using scissors or a small knife, cut each anchovy fillet in half lengthways. Put 2 strips into each pepper wedge. Add a caperberry or a share of the capers to each wedge and sprinkle with the herbs and olive oil.

Roast, uncovered, towards the top of a preheated oven at 180°C (350°F) Gas 4 for 20–30 minutes or until the peppers are wrinkled, aromatic and beginning to char a little at the edges. Serve hot, warm or cool, sprinkled with black pepper.

Note Don't use green peppers for this dish – they lack the sweetness of red or yellow ones.

Both these olive recipes will keep very well in a cool, dark place for weeks – or even months, if they get the chance. *Sott'olio* means 'under oil'. They are excellent served with the crostini on page 12.

black olives
sott'olio

4 tablespoons coriander seeds, crushed

2 tablespoons black peppercorns

8 garlic cloves, halved lengthways

750 g black olives in brine, drained, patted dry and pricked with a fork or sharp knife

zest of 1 large unwaxed lemon, removed in long strips

750 ml extra virgin olive oil

1½ litre preserving jar or 3 x 500 ml jars, sterilized (page 4)

Makes 1 large or 3 small jars

Put the coriander seeds, peppercorns and garlic into a dry frying pan and cook over gentle heat, shaking and toasting until aromatic: do not let them scorch. Stir in the olives and cook for 2–3 minutes.

Put the still-hot sterilized jars onto a folded cloth or wooden board. Using a sterilized spoon, transfer the mixture into the jar(s). Push the lemon zest into the jar(s) with sterilized metal tongs.

Put the oil into a saucepan and heat to 180°C (350°F) or until a small cube of bread turns golden brown in 40 seconds. Let cool for 2 minutes, then pour the oil carefully into the jar(s) to cover the olives. Let cool, uncovered. Top up with any unused oil, cover and seal tightly. Store in a cool, dark cupboard until ready to serve.

If you have fennel flowers in your garden, use the whole seed heads for this dish. Otherwise, use fennel seeds, which are available from most supermarkets.

green olives
with fennel

500 g preserved green olives, washed and dried with kitchen paper, then pricked with a fork

500 ml extra virgin olive oil

2 whole heads of fresh garlic, halved crossways

4–8 fresh fennel flower heads, seeds intact (optional)

3 tablespoons black peppercorns, cracked or coarsely crushed

2 tablespoons fennel seeds

1 teaspoon cloves

1 litre preserving jar or 2 x 500 ml jars, sterilized (page 4)

Makes 1 large or 2 small jars

Pack half the olives loosely into the sterilized jar(s) using sterilized metal tongs or a spoon. Put the olive oil into a saucepan and heat to 180°C (350°F) or until a small cube of bread turns golden brown in 40 seconds. Using a slotted spoon, lower the halved garlic heads and fennel flower heads into the oil. Let them sizzle for about 30 seconds, then lift out and divide between the jar(s). Scatter in the peppercorns, fennel seeds and cloves. Top up with the remaining olives. Pour the hot oil carefully over the olives until covered. Let cool for 2 minutes, then pour the remaining oil carefully into the jar(s) until filled. Let cool, uncovered. Seal tightly and store in a cool, dark cupboard until ready to serve.

This recipe can be served on garlic toasts or with pasta, rice or even polenta. It is delectably easy and good, whichever way you choose. When you buy mussels, keep them cool and use them the same day. Scrub them thoroughly with a small brush and use only those that are tightly closed.

mussels
with garlic, parsley and lemon

1 kg large mussels, scrubbed

4 garlic cloves, chopped

2 tablespoons extra virgin olive oil

100 ml white wine

1 long strip of zest and freshly squeezed juice of 1 lemon

a small bunch of fresh fennel fronds or parsley, chopped

freshly ground black pepper

crusty bread, to serve

Serves 4

Pull off and discard the beards from the mussels. Tap any open mussels against the work surface: if they don't close immediately, discard them. Scrub the mussels briefly and rinse again under cold running water.

Put the mussels into a heavy-based saucepan, add the garlic, olive oil, white wine, lemon zest and juice and bring to the boil. Cover with a lid, reduce the heat to medium and cook, undisturbed, for 3–4 minutes or until the shells are open and the mussels plumply cooked (discard any that don't open).

Stir in half the chopped fennel or parsley, then cover again. Turn off the heat and leave for 1 minute. Remove and discard the empty half-shells from the mussels.

Transfer the mussels into 1 large or 4 small bowls or plates. Sprinkle with the remaining chopped fennel or parsley and lots of black pepper. Eat hot or warm, with crusty bread to mop up the delicious juices.

Variation

Add 1 large tomato, cut into tiny cubes, and omit the lemon zest.

Clams are very popular in Italy and are used in many different ways, all simple and delicious. For instance, *pasta con le vongole* – pasta with clam sauce (page 78) – is an all-time favourite.

clams
with chilli parsley sauce

1 kg small clams, scrubbed, rinsed
and drained

4 tablespoons extra virgin
olive oil

1 teaspoon dried chilli flakes or
crushed chillies

4 garlic cloves, chopped

1 onion, finely chopped

125 ml dry or sweet
white vermouth

freshly ground black pepper

a handful of fresh parsley, chopped,
plus 4–6 leaves, to serve (optional)

Serves 4–6

Put the clams, olive oil, chilli flakes, garlic, onion, vermouth and black pepper into a large saucepan. Bring to the boil, cover tightly with a lid, reduce the heat and let steam for 4–6 minutes.

Stir in the chopped parsley, then cover again. Turn off the heat, let steam for a further 1 minute, then serve, topped with a fresh parsley leaf, if using.

Note Canned or bottled clams in the shell are widely available in Italian delis: useful if you can't find any fresh clams. If using them, drain the liquid into the pan, add all the remaining ingredients except the clams, bring to the boil and reduce to about 250 ml. Add the drained clams, then steam just until the clams have been heated through. Serve as in the main recipe.

White cannellini beans are traditional in Tuscany, but you can use any dried beans. I like chickpeas, and the pretty colour of green flageolets (canned, unripe cannellinis, available in some Italian stores) looks wonderful. Fresh tuna can be expensive, so this recipe is a good way of making one steak stretch a little further.

tonno e fagioli

1 large tuna steak, about 250 g,
or 2 small cans good-quality tuna,
about 160 g each, drained

6 tablespoons olive oil, plus extra for brushing

2 red onions, finely sliced

2–3 fat garlic cloves, crushed

1 tablespoon sherry vinegar or
white wine vinegar

1 kg cooked or canned green flageolet beans,
white cannellini beans, or a mixture of both

4 handfuls of fresh basil leaves
and small sprigs

sea salt and freshly ground black pepper

crusty bread, to serve

a stove-top grill pan

**Serves 6 as a starter,
4 as a main course**

If using fresh tuna, brush with olive oil and put into a preheated stove-top grill pan. Cook for 3 minutes on each side until barred with brown but pink in the centre (the time depends on the thickness of the fish). Remove from the pan, let cool and pull into chunks.

Put the olive oil, onions, garlic and vinegar into a mixing bowl and beat with a fork. Add the beans and, using a metal spoon, toss until well coated.

Add the tuna and basil, then add salt and pepper to taste. Spoon into a serving bowl and serve with crusty bread.

A marvellous, simple chicken salad named after the Gonzagas, who were the Dukes of Mantua, near Modena, the home of balsamic vinegar. True balsamic vinegar is rare and expensive, but you need only a small amount of this rich, sweet dark liquid to transform a dish.

insalata gonzaga

100 g pine nuts

500 g skinless, boneless, roasted chicken breasts

6 tablespoons extra virgin olive oil, preferably from Tuscany or Umbria

1 tablespoon wine vinegar, red or white

2 small red radicchio lettuces, leaves separated

4 tablespoons raisins*

1–2 tablespoons balsamic vinegar

sea salt and freshly cracked black pepper

100 g fresh Parmesan cheese at room temperature, cut into shards, to serve

Serves 4

Put the pine nuts into a dry frying pan and heat gently, stirring, until lightly golden. Remove to a plate and set aside.

Slice the chicken or pull it into shreds. Put the olive oil and vinegar into a salad bowl, add a pinch of salt and beat with a fork. Add the chicken and radicchio and toss gently.

Serve on salad plates, sprinkle with the raisins, pepper and balsamic vinegar and top with shards of fresh Parmesan.

*Note For this salad, I sometimes put the raisins into a bowl and pour over enough verjuice to cover. Soak for 10 minutes before adding to the salad. Verjuice is halfway between vinegar and wine – delicious, if a little difficult to find. You could also soak the raisins in a mixture of 2 tablespoons wine vinegar and 2–4 tablespoons water.

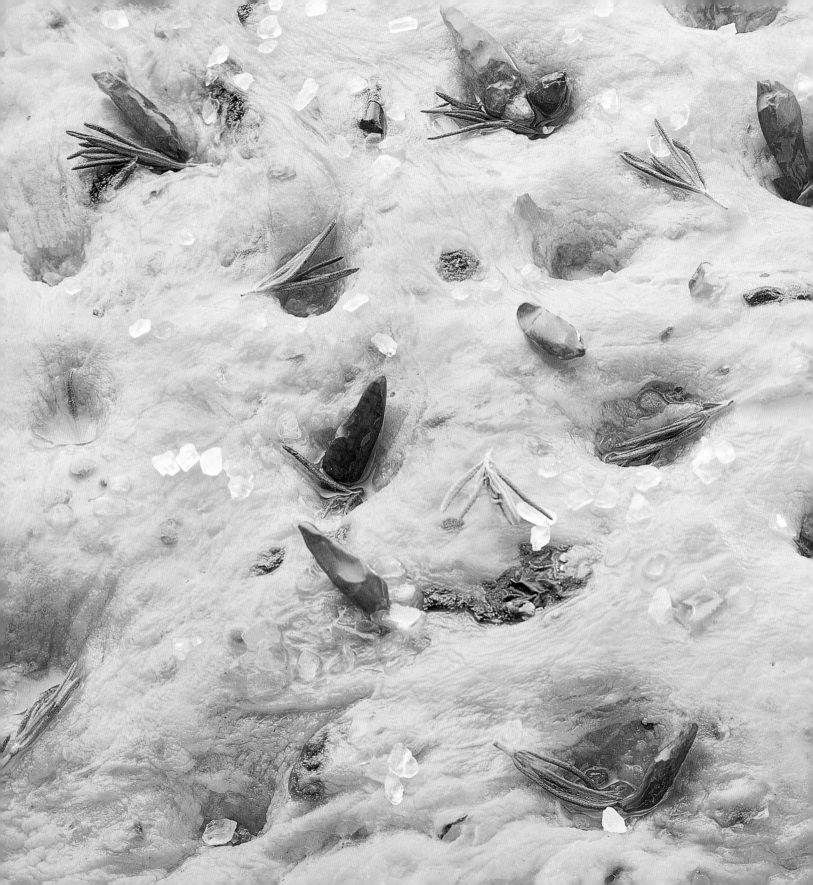

bread
and
pizza

This quick food processor pizza dough also makes excellent focaccia. Olive oil is used in both the rich, flavourful topping and the dough itself – it is delicious as well as authentic and eminently practical, since there is no need to rub the flour into the fat or oil.

focaccia
with olives

1 sachet (7 g) easy-blend dried yeast

250 g plain white flour, plus 4 tablespoons for shaping

½ teaspoon sea salt

2 tablespoons extra virgin olive oil

Topping

finely grated zest and juice of 1 orange

4 tablespoons extra virgin olive oil

2 garlic cloves, crushed

2 tablespoons fresh rosemary leaves, coarsely chopped

½ teaspoon coarsely crushed black pepper

1 teaspoon sea salt flakes or crystals

150 g dry-cured black olives

a large baking sheet, greased

Serves 4

Put the yeast, flour and salt into a food processor fitted with a plastic blade. Pulse briefly to sift the ingredients. Mix the oil and 180 ml warm water together in a small bowl and, with the machine running, pour it in all at once through the feed tube. Process, in short bursts, for 15 seconds until a soft mass forms (not a ball). It will be sticky and soft.

Transfer the dough to a lightly floured work surface, adding the extra 4 tablespoons of flour as you knead. Roll, pat and punch down the dough for 2 minutes, then put the ball of dough into an oiled mixing bowl. Enclose the whole bowl in a large plastic bag. Leave in a warm place until the dough has doubled in size, about 50 minutes.

Transfer the risen dough to a lightly floured work surface, then pat and stretch into a rectangle, about 32 x 22 cm. Transfer to a greased baking tray. Prod the dough all over with your fingertips to form dimples to take the topping.

Put the orange zest and juice, olive oil, garlic, rosemary, black pepper and half the salt into a bowl and, using a wooden spoon, mix well. Pour the mixture over the dough. Scatter with the olives, pushing them well into the dimples. Set aside for 30 minutes to rest the dough.

Bake in a preheated oven at 200°C (400°F) Gas 6 for 25–30 minutes or until crusty and aromatic. Sprinkle with salt. Cut into generous squares, then serve hot or warm.

There isn't much to beat warm, freshly baked focaccia. The key to the lovely, soft texture is to cover the bread with a clean tea towel as soon as it comes out of the oven – the steam will prevent a hard crust forming. You can vary the ingredients by adding chopped olives, tiny cubes of cheese or chopped fresh thyme. Focaccia is best eaten within a day or two of making.

tomato focaccia

500 g tipo 00 or strong white bread flour, plus extra for dusting

1 teaspoon table salt

1 sachet (7 g) easy-blend dried yeast

3 tablespoons olive oil

6 sun-dried tomatoes in oil, drained and chopped

275 ml tepid water

1 teaspoon coarse sea salt

a sprig of fresh rosemary, chopped

2 tablespoons chilli oil

a large baking sheet, greased

Serves 6

Put the flour, table salt and yeast into a large mixing bowl and mix. Make a well in the centre. Add 2 tablespoons of the olive oil, the sun-dried tomatoes and tepid water to the well, then gradually work in the flour to make a soft dough. Sprinkle with a little flour if the mixture feels too sticky, but make sure it's not dry. The dough should be pliable and smooth.

Transfer the dough to a lightly floured work surface and knead for 10 minutes, sprinkling with flour when needed, until the dough is smooth and stretchy.

Rub some olive oil over the surface and return the dough to the mixing bowl. Cover with a clean tea towel and set aside for about 1 hour, until the mixture has doubled in size.

Transfer the risen dough to a lightly floured surface and knead for 2 minutes, until the excess air is knocked out. Roll out the dough to make an oval, about 32 cm long. Carefully set on the prepared baking sheet and cover with a clean tea towel. Set aside for 30 minutes or until almost doubled in size.

Prod the dough all over with your fingertips, to form dimples. Sprinkle with the remaining olive oil, salt and rosemary. Bake in a preheated oven at 200°C (400°F) Gas 6 for about 20–25 minutes until risen and golden.

Remove the focaccia from the oven, cover with a clean cloth and set aside on a wire rack for at least 15 minutes to cool. Drizzle with the chilli oil. Serve warm or at room temperature.

There is nothing better than homemade pizza and once you have tried it, you will never want to buy ready-made again. For a really good pizza dough, try to use the superfine durum wheat 00 flour, which you can buy in Italian stores and large supermarkets. Otherwise, choose a strong white bread flour. You can also add flavourings such as chopped herbs or cheese to the dough.

basic
pizza dough

250 g tipo 00 or strong white bread flour, plus extra for sprinkling

½ teaspoon table salt

1 sachet (7 g) easy-blend dried yeast

2 tablespoons olive oil

125 ml tepid water

Makes 1

1 Put the flour, salt and yeast into a large bowl and mix.

2 Make a well in the centre and add the olive oil and water to the well. Gradually work in the flour to make a soft dough. Sprinkle over a little flour if the mixture feels too sticky, but make sure it is not too dry. The dough should be pliable and smooth.

3 Transfer the dough to a lightly floured work surface and knead for 10 minutes, sprinkling with flour when needed, until the dough is smooth and stretchy. Rub some olive oil over the surface and return the dough to the bowl. Cover with a clean tea towel and set aside for 1 hour, until the dough has doubled in size.

4 Transfer the risen dough to a lightly floured work surface and knead for 2 minutes, until the excess air has been knocked out. Roll out the dough according to the recipe you are following.

Variation

Polenta dough To make a polenta base, use 50 g polenta or fine cornmeal and 200 g strong white bread flour.

Note If you are in a real hurry, there are some good quality packet dough mixes available. Follow the instructions on the packet, but remember to roll it out very thinly.

Roasting peppers is a delicious way to bring out their sweetness. Make sure the peppers are still warm when you add them to the dressing, so they absorb all the flavours of the garlic and parsley.

roasted pepper pizza

2 red peppers
2 yellow peppers
2 garlic cloves, finely chopped
a small bunch of flat leaf parsley, finely chopped
2 tablespoons olive oil
1 recipe pizza dough (page 38)
plain flour, for dusting
1 recipe tomato sauce (page 72)
150 g tomatoes, sliced or halved
150 g mozzarella cheese, drained and sliced
sea salt and freshly ground black pepper

a large baking sheet or pizza baking stone

Makes 1

Put a large baking sheet or pizza stone into the oven at 220°C (425°F) Gas 7 to heat. Put the peppers into a small roasting tin and bake in the preheated oven for 30 minutes, turning them occasionally, until the skins blacken and blister.

Meanwhile, put the garlic and parsley into a small bowl. Add the olive oil, salt and pepper.

Remove the peppers from the oven, cover with a clean tea towel and set aside for 10 minutes or until cool enough to handle but still warm. Pierce the base of each pepper and squeeze the juices into the parsley and oil mixture. Skin and deseed the peppers. Cut the flesh into 2 cm strips and add to the mixture. Cover and set aside at room temperature until needed.

Transfer the pizza dough onto a lightly floured work surface and roll out to 30 cm diameter. Brush with a little olive oil, then spoon over the tomato sauce and arrange the tomatoes and mozzarella cheese on top. Spoon the pepper mixture over the top.

Carefully put it on the hot baking sheet or pizza stone and bake in the preheated oven for about 20–25 minutes until crisp and golden. Using a sharp knife or pizza cutter, cut into wedges and serve.

Bresaola – dried lean beef from the Alpine region of Italy – has a lovely sweetness, which here complements the peppery rocket and salty Parmesan. If you can't find bresaola, use a dry-cured ham, such as serrano or prosciutto instead.

aubergine pizza
with bresaola, rocket and parmesan

1 aubergine, cut into 1 cm slices

3–4 tablespoons olive oil, plus extra to serve

1 recipe pizza dough (page 38)

plain flour, for dusting

1 recipe tomato sauce (page 72)

100 g very finely sliced bresaola or cured ham

50 g fresh rocket leaves

Parmesan cheese, freshly grated or shaved

sea salt and freshly ground black pepper

a large baking sheet or pizza baking stone

a stove-top grill pan

Makes 1

Put a large baking sheet or pizza stone into the oven at 200°C (400°F) Gas 6 to heat. Brush the aubergine slices with the olive oil and sprinkle salt and pepper lightly on both sides. Preheat a stove-top grill pan or large non-stick frying pan over medium heat, add the aubergines and cook for about 3–4 minutes on each side until tender and charred with marks.

Transfer the dough to a lightly floured work surface and roll out to 30 cm diameter. Brush with a little olive oil, then spoon over the tomato sauce and arrange the aubergine slices on top.

Carefully put it on the hot baking sheet or pizza stone and bake in the preheated oven for 15 minutes. Remove from the oven and ripple the bresaola or ham evenly across the pizza. Return the pizza to the oven and bake for a further 5–10 minutes until crisp and golden.

Sprinkle with the rocket, Parmesan, some olive oil and pepper. Using a sharp knife or pizza cutter, cut into wedges and serve.

The pizza for people who just can't make up their minds which one to choose. If you can't find artichokes, use roasted peppers or char-grilled aubergines instead.

quattro stagioni

4 tablespoons olive oil

1 shallot, finely sliced

150 g chestnut mushrooms, sliced

2 tablespoons chopped fresh parsley

1 recipe pizza dough (page 38)

plain flour, for dusting

1 recipe tomato sauce (page 72)

50 g Parma ham, shredded

6 black olives

4 artichoke hearts in brine or oil, drained and quartered

75 g mozzarella cheese, drained and sliced

4 anchovy fillets in oil, drained

sea salt and freshly ground black pepper

fresh basil leaves, to serve

a large baking sheet or pizza baking stone

Makes 1

Put a large baking sheet or pizza stone into the oven at 200°C (400°F) Gas 6 to heat. Heat 2 tablespoons of the oil in a non-stick frying pan, add the shallot and cook for 2 minutes. Add the mushrooms and cook for a further 2–3 minutes until softened and golden. Stir in the parsley, salt and pepper.

Transfer the pizza dough to a lightly floured work surface and roll out to 30 cm diameter. Brush with a little olive oil, then spoon over the tomato sauce. Pile the mushrooms over one-quarter of the pizza. Arrange the ham and olives on another quarter and the artichoke hearts on a third section. Lay the mozzarella on the remaining section and put the anchovies on top.

Sprinkle a little more olive oil, salt and plenty of black pepper over the whole pizza. Carefully put it on the hot baking sheet or pizza stone and bake in the preheated oven for 20–25 minutes until crisp and golden. Using a sharp knife or pizza cutter, cut into quarters, sprinkle the basil over the artichoke portion and serve.

Cooking a pizza upside down is a great way to make sure you get a crisp crust. It also keeps all those sweet tomato juices from escaping – the result is truly spectacular.

topsy turvy
cherry tomato pizza

2–3 tablespoons olive oil

100 g pancetta or unsmoked streaky bacon, cut into cubes

1.25 kg cherry tomatoes

1 recipe pizza dough (page 38)

plain flour, for dusting

juice of 1 lime

2 teaspoons chopped fresh mint

sea salt and freshly ground black pepper

a Swiss roll tin or baking sheet, about 35 x 25 cm

Makes 1

Heat 1 tablespoon of the oil in a non-stick frying pan. Add the pancetta or bacon cubes and cook for 2–3 minutes until golden.

Transfer the pancetta or bacon and the pan oil to a Swiss roll tin or baking sheet. Put the cherry tomatoes into the tin, making sure that they fit in a single layer. Sprinkle with salt and black pepper.

Transfer the dough to a lightly floured work surface and roll out to about the same size as the tin. Put the dough on top of the tomatoes, tucking any overlap inside the tin. Bake in a preheated oven at 200°C (400°F) Gas 6 for about 20–25 minutes until the crust is crisp and dark golden.

Put the lime juice, mint and remaining olive oil into a bowl and mix with a metal spoon.

Carefully invert the pizza onto a chopping board. Drizzle the lime and mint mixture over the top, then cut into slices and serve warm.

The combination of rosemary, pancetta and soft goats' cheese makes a fragrant, summery pizza. This is just as delicious served cool with a pile of leafy salad, making it ideal picnic food.

goats' cheese pizza
with pancetta and rosemary

1 recipe pizza dough
(page 38)

plain flour, for dusting

2 tablespoons olive oil

250 g soft goats' cheese

2 teaspoons coarsely
chopped fresh rosemary

100 g cubed pancetta

sea salt and freshly ground
black pepper

*a large
baking sheet or pizza
baking stone*

Makes 1

Put a large baking sheet or pizza stone into the oven at 200°C (400°F) Gas 6 to heat. Transfer the pizza dough onto a lightly floured work surface and roll out to 30 cm diameter. Brush with 1 tablespoon of the olive oil, then crumble over the cheese and top with the rosemary and pancetta.

Sprinkle the pizza with salt, pepper and the remaining tablespoon of oil. Carefully put it on the hot baking sheet or pizza stone and bake in the preheated oven for 20–25 minutes until crisp and golden. Using a sharp knife or pizza cutter, cut into wedges and serve warm or at room temperature.

A light and crispy pizza with a rather delicate flavour. For a non-vegetarian version, add some Parma ham, bacon or pancetta with the cheese.

wafer potato pizza
with taleggio

1 recipe pizza dough (page 38)

plain flour, for dusting

2 tablespoons olive oil

350 g red-skinned potatoes

6 sage leaves, finely shredded

2 garlic cloves, crushed

200 g Taleggio cheese, chopped

sea salt and freshly ground black pepper

a large baking sheet or pizza baking stone

Makes 4

Put a baking sheet or pizza stone into the oven at 200°C (400°F) Gas 6 to heat.

Divide the dough into 4 pieces and, on a lightly floured work surface, roll each piece into a wafer-thin oval, about 28 cm long. Brush the dough with 1 tablespoon of the olive oil.

Using a mandoline or food processor, cut the potatoes into wafer-thin slices. Put the slices into a mixing bowl, add the sage, garlic and remaining tablespoon of olive oil and, using a metal spoon, toss to coat. Put a single layer of potato slices over each dough base and sprinkle with salt and plenty of black pepper.

Carefully put the pizzas on the hot baking sheet or pizza stone and bake in the preheated oven for 10 minutes. Remove from the oven and dot with the Taleggio. Return to the oven and bake for a further 5–10 minutes until crisp and golden. Serve hot or warm.

The secret of a delicious pizza marinara is the tomatoes. Choose very ripe, plump specimens. It's well worth the extra effort of skinning and deseeding them – the result is a satin-smooth, fragrant and fruity sauce. Don't be tempted to add any cheese!

pizza marinara

3–4 tablespoons olive oil

700 g ripe tomatoes, skinned, deseeded and chopped

1 recipe pizza dough (page 38)

plain flour, for dusting

3 garlic cloves, very finely sliced

1 tablespoon chopped fresh oregano or marjoram

sea salt and freshly ground black pepper

a large baking sheet or pizza baking stone

Makes 1

Put a large baking sheet or pizza stone into a preheated oven at 220°C (425°F) Gas 7 to heat.

Heat 2 tablespoons of the oil in a saucepan and add the tomatoes, salt and pepper. Cook for about 5 minutes, stirring occasionally, until thickened and pulpy.

Transfer the dough to a lightly floured work surface and roll out to 30 cm diameter. Brush with a little olive oil. Spoon over the tomato sauce and sprinkle with the garlic, oregano and a little more olive oil.

Carefully put the pizza on the hot baking sheet or pizza stone and bake in the preheated oven for 15–20 minutes until crisp and golden. Serve hot or cold.

Mushrooms are always an excellent choice for pizza toppings. For a range of flavour and texture use a mixture of varieties, including chestnut, shiitake and field. The basil, chilli and garlic oil isn't essential, but adds quite a boost to the pizza. Some food stores stock a variety of infused oils, such as basil or lemon oil, and these would make a good substitute.

mushroom pizza
with basil, chilli and garlic oil

1 recipe pizza dough (page 38)

plain flour, for dusting

8 tablespoons olive oil

1 recipe tomato sauce (page 72)

400 g mixed mushrooms, thickly sliced

150 g mozzarella cheese, drained and chopped

2 plump garlic cloves, halved

1 large, mild red fresh chilli, deseeded and quartered

8 fresh basil leaves, finely shredded

sea salt and freshly ground black pepper

a large baking sheet or pizza baking stone

Makes 1

Put a large baking sheet or pizza stone into the oven at 220°C (425°F) Gas 7 to heat. Transfer the pizza dough to a lightly floured work surface and roll out to 30 cm diameter. Brush with a little olive oil, then add the tomato sauce, mushrooms and mozzarella.

Sprinkle the pizza with a little olive oil, salt and pepper. Carefully put it on the hot baking sheet or pizza stone and bake in the preheated oven for about 20–25 minutes until crisp and golden.

Meanwhile, put the remaining olive oil into a small saucepan and add the garlic and chilli. Heat very gently for 10 minutes until the garlic is softened and translucent. Remove from the heat and let cool slightly for 5 minutes.

Using a fork, remove and discard the garlic and chilli. Stir the basil into the flavoured oil and sprinkle it over the hot pizza. Using a sharp knife or pizza cutter, cut into wedges and serve hot or warm.

primi
piatti

Whatever kind of cabbage you choose for this soup, make sure you don't cook it any longer than 7–8 minutes. Cabbage doesn't like it, and will punish you with a dreadful stink. Cavolo nero is a dark and delicious Italian variety with white stalks and puckered leaves.

pumpkin bean soup

4 red peppers, halved and deseeded

4 tablespoons olive oil

4 onions, finely sliced

3 garlic cloves, crushed

1.5 kg pumpkin or butternut squash, peeled, deseeded and cut into 2.5 cm cubes or wedges

350 ml chicken stock

200 g cavolo nero or other cabbage, cut into 5 cm pieces

2 cans cannellini beans, 400 g each, rinsed and drained

sea salt and freshly ground black pepper

fresh Parmesan cheese, cut in long shavings, to serve (optional)

Serves 4

Arrange the peppers on a grill rack, skin side up, and cook under a preheated grill until the skins blacken and blister. Transfer to a small saucepan, cover with a lid and let stand for about 5–10 minutes to steam off the skins. Remove from the saucepan and scrape off and discard the skins. Cut each half into 3 pieces and set aside.

Heat the oil in a large, heavy-based saucepan. Add the onions and fry gently until softened and translucent. Add the garlic and fry until golden. Add the pumpkin, toss to coat with the flavoured oil and fry until lightly browned.

Add the stock and bring to the boil. Add the cavolo nero or other cabbage and the reserved peppers, return to the boil, then simmer for about 5 minutes. Stir in the beans, then add salt and black pepper to taste and heat until bubbling. Serve sprinkled with shavings of fresh Parmesan.

Two classic Tuscan soups for the price of one – serve the day it's made, or the next day after reboiling – 'ribollita'. The garlic toast isn't traditional, but helps the soup serve more people. The lettuce added at the end isn't traditional either, but adds an extra crunch.

tuscan ribollita

250 g dried cannellini beans

2 onions (1 cut into 4 wedges through the root, and 1 sliced)

3 carrots (1 cut into quarters lengthways, and 2 sliced)

6 garlic cloves, smashed

6 tablespoons extra virgin olive oil, plus extra for serving

1 fresh red chilli, deseeded and sliced

250 g tomatoes, skinned and chopped

1 leek, sliced

2 celery stalks, finely chopped

sprigs of fresh thyme

3 waxy potatoes, cubed

1 Savoy cabbage or cavolo nero, sliced

sea salt and freshly ground black pepper

Garlic toast

4 tablespoons butter, mashed with 1 crushed garlic clove

8 slices ciabatta bread, toasted

1 cos lettuce, sliced

4 tablespoons chopped fresh flat leaf parsley

Serves 4–6

Put the beans into a bowl and cover with cold water. Soak for 4 hours or overnight.

Drain thoroughly, then put the beans into a heavy-based saucepan with the onion wedges, quartered carrot and half the garlic, cover with water, bring to the boil and simmer until done (the time will depend on the age of the beans, but about 1 hour).

Drain the beans into a large measuring jug, reserving the liquid. Make up to 1.5 litres with water. Remove the flavourings from the beans, then put half the beans into a food processor and process to a coarse purée. Press the purée through a sieve, mouli or potato ricer to remove any bits of bean skin.

Put about 4 tablespoons of the olive oil into a large saucepan, add the sliced onion and cook until softened and translucent. Add the chilli and remaining garlic and cook for a further 5 minutes. Add the tomatoes and puréed beans, then season with salt and pepper. Cook for about 5 minutes, then add the remaining carrots, leek, celery, thyme, potatoes and cabbage. Add the 1.5 litres reserved liquid, bring to the boil and simmer until the vegetables are done, about 20 minutes.

Add the whole beans, then add salt and pepper to taste. Reheat gently and serve immediately or set aside until the next day to make ribollita.

To serve as ribollita, reheat gently, then serve. If you would like to make the soup go further, make garlic toast – spread the garlic butter over the toast and put into 4 large soup bowls. Add the lettuce, ladle the soup over the top and drizzle with olive oil. Sprinkle with chopped fresh parsley and serve.

Zucca is Italian for pumpkin. In Italy, the most common variety is a large squashed globe with a dusty orange skin. Butternut squash makes an acceptable substitute. Even better are those with greenish-blue or grey skins – the flesh is denser, sweeter and less watery. In Italy, the soup is made without potatoes, but they do thicken the soup nicely and smooth the strong, very sweet taste of pumpkin. The milk is important – pumpkin loves milk – and it's also very fond of nutmeg.

zuppa di zucca

1 kg pumpkin, peeled, deseeded and cut into large chunks
2 large potatoes, quartered
1 litre boiling chicken stock or water
50 g unsalted butter
2 tablespoons olive oil
2 large onions, finely sliced
250 ml milk
sea salt

To serve
4 tablespoons sour cream
freshly grated nutmeg
pumpkin crisps (page 90)

Serves 4

Put the pumpkin and potatoes into a large saucepan, add chicken stock or boiling water to cover, then simmer until tender. Drain, reserving the cooking liquid.

Heat the butter and olive oil in a large, non-stick frying pan, add the onions and fry until softened and lightly golden. Transfer to a food processor or blender, then add the pumpkin and potatoes, in batches if necessary. Blend, adding enough milk and cooking liquid to make a thick purée.

Transfer the purée to the saucepan and stir in enough stock to make a thick, creamy soup. Add salt to taste and reheat gently. Ladle the soup into 4 warmed soup bowls, top with sour cream, nutmeg and a few pumpkin crisps, then serve.

Variation

Roasted pumpkin soup For a smoky taste, instead of boiling the pumpkin, roast it in a preheated oven at 225°C (425°F) Gas 7 for about 30–40 minutes until tender.

True minestrone is a thick soup made of chunky vegetables and borlotti beans and either small pasta shapes or rice (especially in the north) – a typical recipe is given below. In summer, the rice-thickened soup can be chilled, like an Italian version of gazpacho. This is a lighter version of the classic soup – more like a broth.

summer minestrone

50 g small dried pasta shapes
1 tablespoon olive oil
1 red onion, chopped
1 garlic clove, finely chopped
2 celery stalks, finely sliced
150 g baby carrots, finely sliced
2 plum tomatoes, coarsely chopped
1.25 litres vegetable stock
150 g runner beans, finely sliced
2 tablespoons Classic Basil Pesto (page 71)
salt and freshly ground black pepper
freshly grated Parmesan cheese, to serve

Serves 4

Bring a large saucepan of water to the boil. Add a good pinch of salt, then add the pasta and cook until *al dente* or according to the instructions on the packet. Drain well.

Meanwhile, heat the olive oil in another large saucepan, add the onion and garlic and cook gently for 3 minutes. Add the celery and carrots and cook for a further 2 minutes. Add the tomatoes and cook for a further 2 minutes.

Add the stock and beans, bring to the boil, then simmer for 5–10 minutes until the vegetables are cooked and tender.

Add the drained pasta, stir in the pesto, then add salt and pepper. Ladle the soup into 4 large, warmed soup bowls, sprinkle with freshly grated Parmesan and serve.

Classic minestrone Use the same vegetables as in the main recipe, but cut them into large chunks, skinning the tomatoes first. Heat 2 tablespoons olive oil or butter in a large saucepan, add 125 g sliced pancetta, the onion and garlic and fry until golden. Add the celery and carrots and sauté until lightly browned. Add 500 g cooked or canned borlotti beans, the runner beans and 2 baking potatoes, cut into chunks. Add 1.25 litres chicken or vegetable stock, the tomatoes and 125 g peas. Bring to the boil, cover and simmer for 2 hours, adding 2 cups tiny pasta or rice for the last 10 minutes. Serve sprinkled with parsley.

A few dried porcini will give a stronger flavour to a soup made with ordinary cultivated mushrooms. Use large, open field mushrooms (portobellos) to give a deeper colour.

mushroom soup
with porcini and parsley

25 g dried porcini mushrooms

4 tablespoons olive oil

6 large, open-capped field mushrooms, wiped, trimmed and sliced

1 onion, halved and finely sliced

3 garlic cloves, crushed

a pinch of freshly grated nutmeg

leaves from a large bunch of fresh parsley, finely chopped in a food processor

1.25 litres boiling chicken stock

4 tablespoons unsalted butter

4 tablespoons plain flour

sea salt and freshly ground black pepper

To serve

4–6 tablespoons coarsely chopped fresh flat leaf parsley

4–6 tablespoons crème fraîche

Serves 4–6

Put the dried porcini into a mixing bowl, add 250 ml boiling water and let soak for 15 minutes. Heat the olive oil in a large, non-stick frying pan, add the fresh mushrooms and sauté gently until browned but still firm.

Add the onion to the frying pan and fry until softened, then add the garlic, nutmeg and parsley. Rinse any grit out of the porcini and strain their soaking liquid several times through muslin to remove any grit. Add the liquid and porcini to the pan (reserve a few small ones for garnish) and bring to the boil.

Reserve a few of the fried mushrooms for serving and transfer the remaining mushroom mixture to a blender. Add 2 ladles of the boiling chicken stock, then blend to a purée.

Heat the butter in a large saucepan, stir in the flour and cook gently, stirring continuously, until the mixture is very dark brown (take care or it will burn). Add the remaining stock, 1 ladle at a time, stirring well after each addition. Add the mushroom mixture, bring to the boil, then simmer for 20 minutes and add salt and pepper to taste. Ladle the soup into warmed soup bowls and serve topped with a few reserved mushrooms, coarsely chopped parsley and a dollop of crème fraîche.

There's something really satisfying about making pasta at home. A food processor and pasta-rolling machine make light work of the job, but you can easily make and roll the dough by hand. You can cut the rolled pasta into strips or use it to make these subtly flavoured ravioli.

fresh filled pasta

300 g pasta flour, such as tipo 00, plus extra for kneading and rolling

a pinch of salt

3 eggs

Pumpkin filling

500 g pumpkin, peeled, deseeded and cut into 5 cm pieces

2 shallots, chopped

4 sage leaves, chopped, plus sprigs to serve

50 g dried breadcrumbs

50 g freshly grated Parmesan cheese

¼ teaspoon freshly grated nutmeg

1 egg

75 g butter, melted

sea salt and freshly ground black pepper

a pasta machine

Makes 500 g dough
Serves 4

1 Put the flour, salt and eggs into a food processor. Process in short bursts until the mixture forms sticky crumbs. Alternatively, to make the dough by hand, sift the flour and into a bowl and make a well in the centre. Add the eggs and, using your hands, gradually work the flour into the eggs. Transfer to a lightly floured work surface and bring together with your hands to form a soft dough. Knead the dough for 5 minutes until it feels smooth, then wrap in clingfilm and chill in the refrigerator for 30 minutes.

2 Divide the pasta dough into 4 pieces, and roll each piece through the pasta machine, going down a setting each time and dusting with flour when necessary. Alternatively, turn out the dough onto a lightly floured work surface and roll out to 2–3 mm thick.

3 To make ravioli, put a sheet of rolled pasta dough onto a lightly floured work surface. Put tablespoons of the filling* in evenly spaced mounds on the dough, leaving about 4 cm between each mound. Cover with a second sheet of rolled pasta dough and, using your fingers, press firmly around the mounds to seal. Using a pasta cutter or sharp knife, cut lines between the mounds to make separate squares, about 8 cm each. Repeat with the remaining pasta dough and filling to make 20 ravioli squares.

4 Bring a large saucepan of water to the boil. Add a good pinch of salt, then add the ravioli and cook for 3–4 minutes until they rise to the surface and are cooked through. Using a slotted spoon, drain carefully and return to the pan. Spoon over melted butter, sprinkle with freshly grated Parmesan and serve.

Note For filled pasta, use each sheet immediately after rolling, or the pasta will dry out. For ribbons or shapes, leave the sheets to dry out on a clean tea towel for 30 minutes before cutting.

***Filling** To make the filling, simmer the pumpkin, shallots and chopped sage in salted water for 8 minutes. Drain, then mash. Stir in the breadcrumbs, cheese and nutmeg. Divide into 16–20 portions.

Pesto is native to Liguria on the Mediterranean coast of north-west Italy. Ligurian basil is said to be more aromatic than any other – but good pesto can also be made with parsley, rocket or sun-dried tomatoes. Most pesto includes nuts, usually pine nuts but occasionally walnuts. It makes a superb, fragrant sauce for pasta, and a delicious addition to a vegetable soup.

classic
basil pesto

50 g fresh basil leaves
2 tablespoons pine nuts
2 garlic cloves
2 tablespoons olive oil
50 g butter, softened
50 g freshly grated Parmesan cheese
freshly ground black pepper

Serves 4

Put the pine nuts into a small, dry frying pan and toast until golden. Let cool.

Put the basil, pine nuts and garlic into a food processor and process until finely chopped. Alternatively, use a mortar and pestle. Add the olive oil, butter, Parmesan and black pepper to taste. Process briefly until blended.

Serve immediately, or transfer to an airtight container or cover with clingfilm and refrigerate for up to 4 days.

Variations

Parsley pesto Use fresh flat leaf parsley instead of basil, and almonds instead of pine nuts.

Rocket pesto Use half rocket and half fresh basil, which gives a bitter edge but tastes curiously good.

This simple sauce is perfect for pasta or as a basic topping for almost any pizza. Choose cans of whole plum tomatoes rather than the chopped sort, which can have a bitter edge. Cook the sauce for at least thirty minutes to give it time to develop some richness. Alternatively, add a pinch of crushed dried chillies to give the sauce an extra kick.

classic
tomato sauce

1 tablespoon olive oil

1 shallot, finely chopped

2 garlic cloves, finely chopped

400 g canned whole plum tomatoes

a sprig of fresh rosemary or thyme, or a pinch of dried oregano

a pinch of sugar

sea salt and freshly ground black pepper

Serves 4

Heat the olive oil in a small saucepan, add the shallot and garlic and cook for 3–4 minutes until softened. Add the tomatoes, breaking them up briefly with a wooden spoon. Add the herbs, sugar, salt and pepper.

Bring the mixture to the boil and part-cover with a lid. Reduce the heat and simmer very gently for 30–60 minutes, stirring from time to time and breaking up the tomatoes with the back of the wooden spoon, until the sauce turns dark red and small droplets of oil appear on the surface.

Discard any woody herb sprigs. Add salt and pepper if necessary, then let cool slightly before using.

Variation

Fiery tomato sauce Put 500 g carton or can of passata or creamed tomatoes, 2 tablespoons olive oil, 2 finely chopped garlic cloves, 6 torn fresh basil leaves, a pinch of crushed dried red chillies and ¼ teaspoon sugar into a small saucepan, with salt and pepper to taste. Proceed as in the main recipe.

One of those simple storecupboard dishes that saves your life when you get home late, tired and hungry. With just four basic ingredients, you can always make this at very short notice.

white spaghetti

150 g dried pasta,
such as spaghetti

6 tablespoons
olive oil

4 garlic cloves,
halved

6 anchovy fillets
in oil, drained

sea salt and freshly
ground black pepper

Serves 2

Bring a large saucepan of water to the boil. Add a good pinch of salt, then add the pasta and cook until *al dente* or according to the directions on the packet.

Put the olive oil and garlic into a small saucepan and heat very gently over a low heat for about 4–5 minutes until the garlic is pale golden but not browned. Remove and discard the garlic.

Add the anchovies and 100 ml water to the saucepan and simmer rapidly, whisking with a fork until the anchovies have almost dissolved. Add pepper and a tiny pinch of salt.

Drain the pasta and return it to the warmed saucepan. Add the anchovy mixture and, using 2 forks, toss well. Spoon the pasta into 2 large serving bowls or plates and serve.

A wonderful combination of two very rich pasta sauces – and absolutely delicious! Make your own fresh pasta from this recipe or the one on page 69, otherwise buy fresh or dried pasta and cook according to the directions on the packet.

fettuccine
with gorgonzola sauce and pesto

Rich pasta dough

250 g Italian flour, tipo 00, or plain flour

2 eggs

2 egg yolks

a pinch of sea salt

Gorgonzola sauce

125 g Gorgonzola or dolcelatte cheese, chopped

125 ml milk

75 ml double cream

25 g unsalted butter

To serve

4 tablespoons Classic Pesto Sauce (page 71) or store-bought

shavings of fresh Parmesan cheese

sprigs of basil

sea salt and cracked black pepper

a pasta machine

Serves 4

Put all the ingredients for the pasta dough into a food processor and process to a dough. Turn out the dough onto a lightly floured work surface and knead until the dough comes together. Roll the pasta dough through a pasta machine according to the manufacturer's instructions. Cut with the fettuccine attachment.

To make the sauce, put the cheese into a small saucepan and melt with the milk, cream and butter. Cook, stirring constantly, until the sauce is thickened, about 5 minutes.*

Bring a large saucepan of water to the boil. Add a good pinch of salt, then add the pasta and cook until it rises to the surface, about 1–2 minutes. If you are using dried pasta, cook until *al dente* or according to the directions on the packet. Drain, then return the pasta to the saucepan, spoon the Gorgonzola sauce over the top and toss gently. Transfer to 4 large, warmed serving bowls, then add the pesto, Parmesan shavings and a sprig of basil. Serve with extra Parmesan, some cracked pepper and a small dish of sea salt.

*Note The pesto can be stirred into the sauce at this point, or spooned on top of the pasta just before serving.

The clams are the real stars of this dish, but it's crucial that the sauce is smooth. If you only have canned tomatoes, purée them with a hand blender or rub them through a sieve before using. Delicious as this is, it's not an elegant meal to eat, so be prepared: tie your napkin firmly round your neck and use your fingers to pick the clams out of their shells. Provide guests with fingerbowls of warm water and a slice of lemon.

pasta con le vongole

2 tablespoons olive oil

2 garlic cloves, finely chopped

a sprig of fresh rosemary

500 ml tomato passata

½ teaspoon sugar

1 kg fresh baby clams or cockles in shells

300 g dried pasta, such as spaghetti or linguine

2 tablespoons chopped fresh flat leaf parsley

salt and freshly ground black pepper

Serves 4

Heat the oil in a saucepan, add the garlic and rosemary and cook over low heat for 2 minutes. Add the passata, sugar, salt and pepper. Bring to the boil, cover with a lid and simmer for 30 minutes. Remove and discard the rosemary.

Put the clams and 2 tablespoons water into a large saucepan. Cover with a lid and cook over medium heat for 4–5 minutes, shaking the pan occasionally until all the shells have opened. Discard any that remain closed. Let cool.

Bring a large saucepan of water to the boil. Add a pinch of salt, then add the pasta and cook until *al dente* or according to the directions on the packet.

Strain the clam cooking juices into a measuring jug, leaving behind any grit. Add the juices to the tomato sauce. Shell half the clams and discard the empty shells. Add the shelled and unshelled clams to the tomato sauce and simmer for 3–4 minutes.

Drain the pasta and return it to the warmed saucepan. Add the clams and chopped parsley and, using 2 forks, toss gently. Spoon the pasta into 4 warmed serving bowls and serve.

This hearty soup of pasta and beans is a classic from the region of Puglia in Italy – the pasta shapes traditionally used are orecchiette, meaning 'little ears'. Try using different pasta shapes, such as fusilli or rotelle if you can't find orecchiette.

pasta e fagioli

2 tablespoons olive oil

1 small onion, finely chopped

2 garlic cloves, finely chopped

1 potato, chopped

2 ripe tomatoes, coarsely chopped

1.25 litres chicken or vegetable stock

a sprig of fresh thyme, sage or rosemary

800 g canned cannellini beans, drained

150 g small dried pasta shapes, such as orecchiette

a pinch of crushed dried chillies

sea salt and freshly ground black pepper

freshly grated Parmesan cheese, to serve

Serves 4

Heat the olive oil in a large saucepan, add the onion, garlic and potato and cook for 3–4 minutes until golden. Add the tomatoes and cook for 2–3 minutes until softened.

Add the stock, a herb sprig, the beans, pasta, dried chillies, salt and pepper. Bring to the boil and simmer for about 10 minutes until the pasta and potatoes are cooked.

Ladle the soup into 4 large, warmed soup bowls and serve sprinkled with Parmesan.

Variations

• Use fresh shelled broad beans instead of the cannellini beans

• Substitute 1 fresh red chilli, finely chopped, for the crushed dried chillies

• Use different pasta shapes, such as fusilli, rotelle or conchiglie or use small soup pasta, such as anellini or ditali.

An ever-popular Italian dish – perfect for any occasion from an informal gathering to a special dinner party. Serve the lasagne with a crisp salad and crusty bread.

baked lasagne

500 g dried lasagne

300 g mozzarella cheese, drained and chopped

4 tablespoons freshly grated Parmesan cheese

salt and freshly ground black pepper

Bolognese sauce

10 g dried porcini mushrooms, rinsed

1 tablespoon olive oil

1 onion, finely chopped

500 g beef mince

50 g Parma ham, coarsely chopped

100 ml Marsala or sherry

700 ml passata or sieved tomatoes

White sauce

1 litre milk

1 small garlic clove

50 g butter

50 g plain flour

a baking dish, about 30 x 20 x 7 cm, lightly oiled

Serves 8

To make the bolognese sauce, put the dried porcini into a bowl, pour over enough boiling water to cover and let soak for 20 minutes until softened. Heat the olive oil in a large saucepan, add the onion and cook for 2 minutes. Add the beef and Parma ham and cook for 3–4 minutes, stirring constantly, until evenly browned. Drain the porcini and discard the soaking water. Chop the porcini, then add to the pan with the Marsala and passata. Cover with a lid and simmer for 1 hour, stirring occasionally, until rich and dark. Add salt and black pepper to taste.

Bring a large saucepan of water to the boil. Add a good pinch of salt, then add the lasagne sheets, one at a time, so that they don't stick together. Cook for 5 minutes, then drain and tip the lasagne into a bowl of cold water. Drain again and pat dry with kitchen paper.

To make the white sauce, put the milk and garlic into a small saucepan and heat gently until warm. Melt the butter in a separate saucepan, then stir in the flour and cook for 1 minute. Gradually add the warm milk, stirring constantly to make a smooth sauce. Bring to the boil, then simmer for 2–3 minutes. Remove and discard the garlic clove. Add salt and black pepper to taste.

Put 3–4 tablespoons of the bolognese sauce into the baking dish, spread evenly across the base of the dish with a spoon, then cover with a layer of lasagne. Spoon over some white sauce and a few pieces of mozzarella and continue adding layers, starting with another layer of bolognese sauce and finishing with the white sauce and mozzarella, until all the ingredients have been used. Sprinkle with black pepper and freshly grated Parmesan, then bake in a preheated oven at 190°C (375°F) Gas 5 for about 30 minutes until the top is crusty and golden.

There are a number of different kinds of gnocchi or dumplings. These, made with cooked mashed potato, are the most common. Others are made with semolina (page 85), pumpkin or leftover rice. All are incomparable.

gnocchi
with tomato sauce

1 kg large floury potatoes

a pinch of sea salt

2 egg yolks

200 g plain flour, plus extra for rolling

1 litre boiling water, or beef or chicken stock, for poaching

To serve

500–750 ml Classic Tomato Sauce (page 72)

a handful of fresh basil leaves

1 tablespoon chopped fresh chives

freshly grated Parmesan cheese (optional)

sea salt and freshly ground black pepper

Serves 4–8

To make the gnocchi, bring a large saucepan of lightly salted water to the boil. Add the potatoes and cook until soft. Drain and either mash with a potato masher or press through a potato ricer into a large bowl. Add the salt and, using a fork, beat the egg yolks and flour into the potatoes, a little at a time, to form a smooth, slightly sticky dough.

Transfer the dough to a well floured board and roll out into cylinders, about 1 cm in diameter. Cut each piece into sections, about 2 cm long. Put each piece on the back of a fork, press down with your thumb and roll or flick the piece off the end of the fork onto the floured board, leaving grooves on one side of the gnocchi – the grooves will help hold the sauce.

Pour the boiling water or stock into a large saucepan, return to the boil, add the gnocchi about 20 at a time, and cook until they rise to the surface. Simmer for a further 50–60 seconds until cooked through, then, using a slotted spoon, transfer to a large bowl. Repeat until all the gnocchi are cooked.

To serve, spoon a pool of the tomato sauce into 4 wide soup bowls, then add the gnocchi. Sprinkle with fresh basil leaves, chopped chives, salt and pepper. If using grated Parmesan, serve separately.

Semolina-based gnocchi are made from a stiff dough that can be cut out with a biscuit cutter. They can be baked until crusty, with two kinds of cheese clinging in delicious golden strands. These are really addictive – all you need is a glass of wine and a cool, green salad for contrast.

oven-baked
semolina gnocchi

2 tablespoons extra virgin olive oil

8 tablespoons coarse semolina, about 90 g, plus extra for shaping

100 g freshly grated Parmesan cheese

100 g freshly grated or finely cubed Gruyère cheese

a handful of fresh flat leaf parsley, coarsely chopped

¼ teaspoon grated nutmeg

¼–½ teaspoon crumbled dried red chilli (optional)

sea salt

4 tablespoons extra virgin olive oil, for serving

a plain biscuit cutter, 5 cm diameter

a small baking dish, lightly oiled

Serves 2–3

Put 250 ml warm water into a large bowl. Add the olive oil, ½ teaspoon salt and semolina in that order and, using an electric or balloon whisk, whisk until well mixed. The oil helps avoid lumps, but work quickly.

Pour the mixture into a large, non-stick frying pan and cook over medium heat, stirring constantly with a wooden spoon until the mixture thickens and forms a paste, about 3 minutes. It will come away from the sides of the pan.

Stir in half the Parmesan and half the Gruyère, and the parsley, nutmeg and chilli, if using. Transfer the paste to a work surface dusted with semolina and, using your hands, pat and smooth out to a 20 cm square. Using a 5 cm biscuit cutter, cut out 16 rounds. Lift them out carefully with a spatula.

Arrange in the prepared baking dish in overlapping concentric circles or rows. Sprinkle with the remaining Parmesan and Gruyère and half the olive oil. Bake in a preheated oven at 200°C (400°F) Gas 6 for about 30–35 minutes until hot, crusty and aromatic. Serve immediately, drizzled with the remaining olive oil.

Italians adore their pasta, but they also love risotto. Quick to prepare, nutritious, inexpensive and utterly delicious, risotto is also very versatile – perfect for relaxed, weekday meals or smart dinner parties.

basic
risotto

2 tablespoons extra virgin olive oil

25 g unsalted butter

1 onion, sliced

275 g risotto rice such as vialone nano, carnaroli or arborio

½ teaspoon sea salt

900 ml boiling chicken or vegetable stock

flavourings of your choice

Serves 4

1 Heat the oil and butter in a wide saucepan. Add the onion and sauté for 2 minutes until softened and translucent.

2 Add the rice and stir with a wooden spoon until the grains are well coated and glistening with oil, about 1–2 minutes.

3 Add the salt and one-third of the boiling stock and bring to the boil. Simmer, stirring, until all the liquid has been absorbed. Continue to add the stock at intervals and cook at a steady simmer, stirring, until all the liquid has been absorbed and the rice is tender, but firm or *al dente* in the centre. If you run out of stock, use boiling water to complete cooking the rice.

4 Mix in flavourings of your choice, such as quartered artichoke hearts, sautéed mushrooms and chicken livers, chopped chives, chopped flat leaf parsley and freshly grated Parmesan.

Pumpkin aficionados always use varieties with green or grey skins: they are drier and denser than common pumpkins and butternut squash, giving a more intense flavour and better texture. Italian pumpkin has pale, orange-brown skin.

pumpkin risotto

about 700 g pumpkin or butternut squash, peeled, deseeded and cut into large chunks (500 g after preparation)

2 potatoes, peeled and cut into large chunks (optional)

25 g salted butter

milk (optional – see method)

1 litre chicken stock

4 tablespoons olive oil

2 onions, finely chopped

2 fat garlic cloves, crushed

400 g risotto rice

sea salt and freshly ground black pepper

To serve (optional)

shavings of fresh Parmesan cheese

pumpkin crisps*

Serves 4

Put the pumpkin and potatoes, if using, into a large saucepan and cover with water. Bring to the boil, then simmer until tender. Drain thoroughly and mash with half the butter until creamy – it should have the consistency of thick soup (add milk if necessary).

Put the stock into a large saucepan and heat until almost boiling, then reduce the heat until barely simmering to keep it hot.

Heat the olive oil and remaining butter in a heavy sauté pan, add the onions and fry gently until softened and translucent. Add the garlic and cook until lightly golden, about 1–2 minutes. Add the rice and stir with a wooden spoon, until the grains are well coated with oil, about 1–2 minutes. Add a ladle of the boiling stock and simmer gently, stirring, until all the liquid has been absorbed. Continue to add the stock at intervals and cook at a steady simmer, stirring, until the liquid has been absorbed and the rice is tender, but firm or *al dente* in the centre. Stir the cooked pumpkin through the risotto, season to taste and serve, topped with shavings of Parmesan and pumpkin crisps.

*Pumpkin crisps To make pumpkin crisps, finely slice segments of pumpkin on a mandoline or with a vegetable peeler (include the skin). Fill a wok or deep-fat fryer one-third full of oil, or to the manufacturer's recommended level. Add the slices of pumpkin, in batches if necessary, and fry until crisp. Remove with a slotted spoon and drain thoroughly on kitchen paper.

This fragrant, golden risotto is an Italian classic, to serve on its own or as an accompaniment to Osso Buco (page 110). The original *risotto alla milanese* includes beef marrow, which makes it extra-rich.

saffron risotto

1 litre chicken stock

75 g salted butter

1 onion, sliced

3–4 garlic cloves, crushed (optional)

450 g risotto rice, such as vialone nano, carnaroli or arborio

125 ml white wine

a large pinch of saffron threads

¼ teaspoon sea salt (or, if stock is salty, sugar)

75 g fresh Parmesan cheese, shaved with a vegetable peeler

freshly ground black pepper

sprigs of flat leaf parsley, to serve

Serves 4

Put the stock into a large saucepan, heat until almost boiling, then reduce the heat until barely simmering to keep it hot.

Heat 50 g of the butter in a saucepan, add the onion and garlic, if using, and sauté gently for 1 minute. Add the rice and stir with a wooden spoon, until the grains are well coated and glistening with oil, about 1–2 minutes. Add the wine and stir until completely absorbed.

Put the saffron and salt or sugar into a small bowl and, using a wooden spoon, grind together, then add 1 ladle of the hot stock. Pour half this mixture into the rice and reserve the remainder. Continue to add the stock at intervals and cook at a steady simmer, stirring, until all the liquid has been absorbed and the rice is tender, but firm or *al dente* in the centre, 25–30 minutes. Alternatively, add all the stock at once and cook over a low heat for about 30 minutes, stirring gently from time to time.

Add the remaining butter and saffron, then stir in half the Parmesan and some black pepper. To serve, sprinkle with the remaining cheese and top with sprigs of parsley.

Variation

Wild mushroom risotto Put 25 g broken dried porcini mushrooms and 15 g broken dried morel mushrooms into a saucepan and add 1 litre boiling chicken stock. Simmer, covered, for 10–15 minutes until dark and flavourful. Strain the liquid and set aside. Rinse the mushroom pieces under cold running water. Proceed as in the main recipe, but use red wine instead of white, and omit the saffron and salt or sugar. The mushrooms should be cooked with the rice.

This risotto is light, fresh and vibrantly green – a reminder of early summer, when asparagus and peas grow in abundance. Try to use vegetables when they are in season, so that you can enjoy them at their finest and sweetest.

risotto
with asparagus, peas and basil

900 ml vegetable stock

50 g unsalted butter

1 tablespoon olive oil

8 shallots, finely chopped

275 g risotto rice, such as vialone nano, carnaroli or arborio

75 ml white wine

350 g asparagus, cut into 4 cm lengths

150 g fresh or frozen shelled peas

finely grated zest of 1 unwaxed lemon

100 g freshly grated Parmesan cheese, plus extra to serve

a large handful of fresh basil, leaves torn, plus extra to serve

sea salt and freshly ground black pepper

Serves 4

Put the stock into a large saucepan and heat until almost boiling, then reduce the heat until barely simmering to keep it hot.

Heat the butter and oil in a large sauté pan or casserole. Add the shallots and cook for 1–2 minutes until softened and translucent.

Add the rice and stir with a wooden spoon, until the grains are well coated and glistening with oil, about 1–2 minutes. Pour in the wine and stir until it has been completely absorbed.

Add 1 ladle of hot stock and simmer, stirring, until it has been absorbed. Repeat. After 10 minutes, add the asparagus, peas and lemon zest and mix well. Continue to add the stock at intervals and cook at a steady simmer until all the liquid has been absorbed and the rice is tender, but firm or *al dente* in the centre, about 8–10 minutes.

Add the Parmesan and basil, then add salt and black pepper to taste. Mix well. Remove from the heat, cover and let rest for 2 minutes.

Spoon into 4 large, warmed bowls and top with fresh basil leaves and extra Parmesan, if using. Serve immediately.

Try to buy young artichokes with long, uncut stems. The shorter the stem, the tougher the artichoke tends to be. Firmly closed artichokes are an indication of freshness: if the leaves are open they are old.

artichoke risotto

4 small or 2 large globe artichokes
1 lemon, halved
900 ml vegetable stock
50 g unsalted butter
1 tablespoon olive oil
8 shallots, finely chopped
1 garlic clove, crushed
275 g risotto rice, such as vialone nano, carnaroli or arborio
75 ml white wine
100 g freshly grated Parmesan cheese, plus extra to serve
2 tablespoons mascarpone cheese
a handful of fresh flat leaf parsley, coarsely chopped
sea salt and freshly ground black pepper

Serves 4

To prepare the artichokes, pull off the tough outer leaves and cut off the spiky, pointed top with a sharp knife. Remove the stalk and cut each artichoke lengthways into 4 segments if small or 8 segments if large. Cut away the fuzzy, prickly choke. Squeeze the lemon over the segments to prevent discoloration. Set the artichoke segments aside.

Put the stock into a saucepan and heat until almost boiling, then reduce the heat until barely simmering and keep it hot.

Heat the butter and oil in a heavy sauté pan or casserole over medium heat. Add the shallots and cook for 1–2 minutes until softened but not browned. Add the garlic and artichoke segments and cook for 2–3 minutes.

Add the rice and stir with a wooden spoon, until the grains are well coated and glistening with oil, about 1–2 minutes. Pour in the wine and stir until completely absorbed.

Add a ladle of hot stock and simmer, stirring, until it has been absorbed. Continue to add the stock at intervals and cook as before until the liquid has been absorbed and the rice is tender, but firm or *al dente* in the centre, about 18–20 minutes in total.

Add the Parmesan, mascarpone and parsley, then add salt and pepper to taste. Mix well. Remove from the heat, cover and let rest for 2 minutes. Spoon into 4 warmed serving bowls and serve immediately with freshly grated Parmesan.

This is a dual-purpose risotto recipe: the first section will produce a traditional saffron risotto – slightly different from the one on page 92 – and is served hot. If you let it cool, it can be used to make this unusual risotto cake. Both are flavoured and coloured with saffron. Saffron threads are best, but Italian delicatessens sell very good quality saffron powder in little sachets – just add it to the boiling stock and proceed as usual (the threads must be steeped in boiling water first).

italian risotto cake

Saffron risotto

50 g salted butter

6 tablespoons extra virgin olive oil

2 leeks, white only, finely sliced

4 garlic cloves, chopped

300 g Italian risotto rice

a large pinch saffron threads, soaked in 60 ml boiling water for 10 minutes

1 litre hot chicken or veal stock

50 g freshly grated Parmesan cheese

sea salt, to taste

Risotto cake

450 g cooked, cooled saffron risotto

1 egg yolk, beaten

1 egg, beaten

75 g mozzarella cheese, chopped

2–3 tablespoons extra virgin olive oil

To serve

freshly cracked black pepper

shavings of fresh Parmesan cheese

rocket, watercress or red chicory

Serves 4

Put the stock into a large saucepan, heat until almost boiling, then reduce the heat until barely simmering to keep it hot.

To make the risotto, heat the butter and olive oil in a large heavy-based saucepan. Add the leek and garlic and cook gently until softened and translucent. Add the rice and cook, stirring, for about 1–2 minutes until the grains are well coated and glistening with oil. Add all the saffron and its soaking water, then the stock, 1 ladle at a time, and simmer until each ladle is absorbed before adding the next. Stir in the Parmesan and salt and serve immediately, or let cool and use to make the risotto cake.

To make the risotto cake, put the cold rice, egg yolk, egg and chopped mozzarella into a bowl and mix carefully – it must be thoroughly amalgamated, but the rice grains should not be broken.

Heat the oil until very hot in a large non-stick frying pan, tilting the pan so the oil covers the sides as well as the base. Spoon in the rice mixture, smooth the top and cook over medium heat for 6–8 minutes or until the base is golden and there is a strong aroma. (Take care that it doesn't burn.) Put a flat saucepan lid or large plate on top and invert the frying pan and plate in one quick movement. Slide the rice back in, crust up, and cook the second side until golden.

To serve, cut the cake into wedges. Serve hot or warm, sprinkled with cracked pepper, shavings of Parmesan and crisp leaves such as rocket, watercress or red chicory.

secondi piatti

A great dish with assertive flavours suitable for any occasion. Alter the composition of this soup-stew according to what's available in your local market, but include thick white fish, shellfish and prawns. Serve with fresh Italian bread and a jug of light red wine or the peppery white wine from the Vesuvius area around the Bay of Naples.

neapolitan
seafood stew

4 large garlic cloves, crushed

a bunch of fresh thyme or rosemary

12 clams or other bivalves

12 mussels

about 4 tablespoons olive oil

2 large onions, cut into wedges through the root

8 ripe, very red tomatoes, skinned, halved and deseeded

1 kg thick boneless white fish fillets, such as cod

4–8 small whole fish, cleaned and scaled (optional)

8 uncooked prawns

1 litre boiling fish stock

sea salt and freshly ground black pepper

crusty Italian bread, to serve

Serves 4

Put 250 ml water into a large saucepan and add 1 crushed garlic clove and half the herbs. Bring to the boil, then simmer for 2–3 minutes to extract the flavours. Add the clams, cover with a lid and cook over high heat, shaking the pan from time to time. As they open, remove and put onto a plate, so they don't overcook. Discard any that don't open.

Add the mussels to the pan, cover with a lid and cook until they open. Remove as they do so and add to the plate with the clams. Discard any that don't open. Strain the cooking stock through muslin into a bowl to remove the grit. Set aside.

Heat the olive oil in a large frying pan, add the onion wedges and cook until lightly browned on both sides. Reduce the heat and cook until softened. Stir in the remaining garlic and cook for a few minutes until golden. Add lots of black pepper, then add the tomatoes, the remaining herbs, both kinds of fish and the prawns. Pour in the stock and bring to boiling point. Reduce the heat and simmer for a few minutes until the fish turns opaque. Add the mussels, clams and the strained mussel poaching liquid. Reheat, then add salt and pepper.

Ladle into 4 large, warmed bowls and serve with crusty Italian bread.

A taste of the Mediterranean – whole fish or fillets wrapped in foil and barbecued until tender, served with olive oil flavoured with garlic, capers, lemon juice and anchovy – an intense effect that's not for the faint-hearted!

sea bass parcels

4 medium sea bass or snapper, about 300 g each, or 4 fillets, 150 g each

freshly squeezed juice of 1 lemon, plus extra to taste

125 ml extra virgin olive oil

8 canned anchovy fillets, chopped

2 garlic cloves, chopped

4 tablespoons tiny pickled capers, drained

a small handful of fresh flat leaf parsley, chopped

sea salt and freshly ground black pepper

4 sheets of foil, 25 cm wide, brushed with oil

a large baking sheet

Serves 4

Using a sharp knife, make 2–3 diagonal slashes in both sides of each fish and rub in salt and black pepper. Set each fish onto a sheet of oiled foil and sprinkle with half the lemon juice. Take the long edges of foil and pinch and roll together to form a tight seal. Loosely pleat or fold the foil lengthways, then crunch and roll the narrow ends until tightly closed. Put the parcels onto a large baking sheet.

Bake the parcels in a preheated oven at 180°C (350°F) Gas 4 for 10–15 minutes for fillets or about 20–25 minutes for whole fish, or until the flesh is white and firm (open one parcel to test). Alternatively, cook on a preheated barbecue over medium-hot coals for 8–12 minutes for whole fish or 6–8 minutes for fillets.

Meanwhile, put the remaining lemon juice, olive oil, anchovies and garlic into a blender and process to form a purée. Alternatively, use a pestle and mortar. Pour the mixture into a mixing bowl, then stir in the capers and parsley. Add extra lemon juice to taste.

Put the fish parcels onto 4 large, warmed serving plates. Open each one just enough to drizzle with the sauce, then reseal and serve.

For the best flavour and texture, choose a free-range bird for this dish. You can roast it first on one side, then the other, then breast up for the final stage. Don't worry about the amount of garlic — when it's roasted like this, it becomes sweet and nutty.

italian roast chicken

1.25–1.5 kg free-range or organic chicken

25 g unsalted butter, about 2 tablespoons

4 garlic cloves, well crushed, plus 4 whole heads of garlic (optional)

melted butter or olive oil, for brushing

6 tablespoons robust red wine, such as Cabernet Sauvignon, Shiraz (Syrah) or Pinot Noir

sea salt and freshly ground black pepper

Serves 4

Using your fingers, work the skin of the chicken loose over the breast and thighs. Wiggle the wishbone free and cut it out, trying not to puncture the skin. This will make it easier to carve.

Put the butter and crushed garlic into a small mixing bowl and blend well. Push some of the mixture under the breast skin and leg skin. Skewer the neck skin closed underneath. Season the bird all over with salt and black pepper. Slice the tops off the whole heads of garlic, if using, cutting them part-way through, and brush them all over with melted butter or olive oil. Set aside.

Set the bird in a large roasting tin, or on a roasting rack in the tin. Roast in a preheated oven at 220°C (425°F) Gas 7 for 45 minutes, then add the whole garlic heads and reduce the oven temperature to 190°C (375°F) Gas 5. Roast for a further 30 minutes. To test the chicken, pierce the thigh in the thickest part with a skewer. The juices should run clear and golden. If the juices still look at all pink, cook a little longer.

Transfer the chicken to a large serving dish, add the whole roasted garlic, if using, and put the dish into the oven. Turn off the heat and leave the door slightly open. Set the roasting tin on top of the stove over a high heat and stir in the wine, scraping up all the sediment from the base of the tin. Boil down until syrupy. Serve this simple sauce with the roast chicken. The sweet, soft, roasted garlic cloves should be squeezed out of their papery coatings and eaten with the chicken.

Polpette – meatballs – are made all over Italy using finely minced lamb, beef, veal or pork with whatever accents suit them best: cheese, herbs, sausage, capers, citrus zest, pine nuts, chilli and even anchovy. In Sicily, lemon leaves are common, but you can substitute grated or finely sliced lemon zest. Before cooking, either roll the meatballs in grated zest, or insert sliced zest.

polpette al limone

450 g lean lamb, minced twice

250 g luganega or other coarse Italian sausage, removed from its casing

2 slices of stale Italian bread, about 75 g

beef stock or water, for dipping the bread

1 egg, beaten

1 small handful of flat leaf parsley, chopped

4 garlic cloves, chopped

½ teaspoon ground allspice, mace or nutmeg

1 teaspoon sea salt

6 tablespoons freshly grated Parmesan cheese

freshly ground black pepper

24 fresh lemon leaves (optional)

juice and zest of 1 lemon (see method)

6–8 tablespoons olive oil, for frying

stock, wine or water, to deglaze the pan

creamy mashed potato, to serve

24 wooden cocktail sticks

Serves 4

Put the lamb and sausage meat into a large bowl and, using a wooden spoon, mix thoroughly. Put the bread into another bowl, pour over the stock or water and let soak for 2 minutes. Squeeze dry and crumble in with the meats. Add the beaten egg, parsley, garlic, spice, salt, cheese and black pepper. Beat and knead to a smooth paste, then using wet (or oiled) hands, divide into 24 balls. Pinch and squeeze to make them compact, then flatten slightly. If using lemon leaves, fasten one onto each ball with a cocktail stick. Alternatively, roll the balls in grated lemon zest or insert a strip of zest.

Heat half the olive oil in a large, non-stick frying pan. Add half the polpette and sauté for about 2–3 minutes on each side until golden, firm and aromatic. Remove from the pan, keep hot and repeat with the remaining olive oil and polpette. Squeeze the juice of the lemon into the frying pan and add a little stock, wine or water to dissolve the pan sediment. Pour the pan juices over the polpette and serve with creamy mashed potato.

Well-cooked osso buco, braised shin of veal, is so tender it can be eaten with a spoon. *Oss bus* in Milanese dialect means 'bone with a hole' – inside the hole is the creamy bone marrow that's the choicest part of the dish. Get your butcher to cut chunks of the hind shin, about 5 cm thick, then tie up the pieces with string so the marrow doesn't fall out during cooking. This authentic version doesn't contain tomatoes – it is flavoured instead with anchovy and sprinkled with gremolata, made from lemon zest, parsley and garlic.

osso buco

8 pieces of shin of veal, 5 cm thick (tied up with string to keep in the marrow)

75 g plain flour, seasoned with salt and pepper

6 tablespoons extra virgin olive oil

50 g unsalted butter

2 onions, sliced into rings

2 carrots, chopped or sliced

2 celery stalks, chopped or sliced

6 salted or 8 canned anchovies, rinse and chopped

250–500 ml white wine

250 ml veal, beef or chicken stock

a small bunch of fresh herbs, such as parsley, thyme, bay leaf and lovage tied together

sea salt and freshly ground black pepper

Gremolata topping

finely grated zest of ½ lemon

a small bunch of fresh flat leaf parsley, chopped

2 garlic cloves, crushed

Serves 4–6

Choose a flameproof casserole or lidded frying pan into which the meat will fit snugly. Put the meat onto a board and dust with the flour on both sides. Heat the olive oil in the casserole or frying pan. Add the meat and brown for 5 minutes on each side, turning carefully.

Heat the butter in another frying pan. Add the onions, carrots and celery and brown for a few minutes. Add the anchovies and mash with a wooden spoon. Add the wine and let bubble for about 2 minutes.

Lift up the meat with a slotted spoon, add half the vegetable-anchovy mixture underneath. Put the veal on top and pour over the remaining vegetable-anchovy mixture. Trickle the stock down the sides of the pan until the meat is nearly covered, then add the bunch of fresh herbs. Bring to the boil, cover, reduce the heat to very low and simmer for 1½–2 hours on top of the stove. Alternatively, bake in a preheated oven at 150°C (300°F) Gas 2 for 2½ hours.

To make the gremolata, put the lemon zest, parsley and garlic into a bowl and mix well. When the meat is tender, cut the string and serve the pieces in large, warmed soup plates. Spoon some of the sauce over each helping, then add the gremolata topping.

Variation

This recipe can also be made with lamb shanks. Allow 1–2 shanks per person, depending on size.

This elegant dish combines rich and fascinating flavours – beef, truffle oil, thyme, garlic and full-flavoured flat mushrooms. The sliced rare beef is set on a pleasantly peppery salad. Really good estate-bottled extra virgin olive oil is crucial – together with earthy, distinctive truffle oil, it transforms this dish into a gourmet event.

char-grilled beef fillet
with field mushrooms

4 fillet steaks, 250 g each, well aged, at room temperature

6 tablespoons extra virgin olive oil

2 tablespoons truffle oil

1 tablespoon sherry vinegar

1 teaspoon black peppercorns, coarsely crushed

a small bunch of fresh thyme sprigs

4 large open mushrooms

2 garlic cloves, crushed

sea salt flakes, crushed

Salad

2 handfuls of rocket leaves

2 handfuls of watercress

2 handfuls of lamb's lettuce

100 g red radishes, sliced crossways

100 g fresh Parmesan cheese, cut into long shavings with a vegetable peeler

a stove-top grill pan

Serves 4

Pat the beef dry with kitchen paper. Put it into a plastic bag, add 3 tablespoons of the olive oil, the truffle oil, vinegar, crushed peppercorns and thyme. Using your fingers, knead gently together. Seal the bag loosely and set aside to marinate in the refrigerator for 30 minutes.

To make the salad, put the rocket, watercress, lamb's lettuce, radishes and Parmesan into a large bowl and toss gently. Pile onto 4 serving plates and drizzle with the remaining olive oil.

Remove the beef from the bag, drain, then put into a preheated stove-top grill pan or large, non-stick frying pan. Alternatively, cook on a preheated barbecue over medium-hot coals. Put the mushrooms into the plastic bag, add the garlic and 1 teaspoon of crushed sea salt flakes and, using your fingers, turn until the marinade is evenly absorbed.

Cook the fillets for 5–6 minutes on each side or until well marked in lines, aromatic and dark, but still pink inside. Transfer to a large, warmed plate and let stand, covered, while you cook the mushrooms.

Add the mushrooms to the pan or barbecue and cook for 2–3 minutes on each side or until dark and aromatic. (If any marinade is left in the bag, pour it into the cupped side of the mushrooms first.)

To serve, slice each fillet crossways into 5–6 slices. Arrange the sliced fillets on top of the salad. Add the mushrooms, halved or quartered, then serve.

contorni

There are as many variations of this Tuscan bread salad as there are cooks. The secret is to let the flavours blend well without the bread disintegrating into a mush. Always use the ripest, reddest, most flavourful tomatoes you can find: Italian plum tomatoes, the big ones with furrowed skin and heritage varieties like Black Russian all work well in this dish.

tuscan panzanella

6 very ripe plum tomatoes

2 garlic cloves, finely sliced

200 ml extra virgin olive oil

4 thick slices day-old bread, preferably Italian-style such as puglièse or ciabatta

10 cm cucumber, halved, deseeded and finely sliced diagonally

1 red onion, chopped

1 tablespoon chopped fresh flat leaf parsley

2 tablespoons white wine vinegar, cider vinegar or sherry vinegar

1 teaspoon balsamic vinegar (optional)

a bunch of fresh basil, leaves torn

12 caperberries or 4 tablespoons capers packed in brine, rinsed and drained

sea salt and freshly ground black pepper

a baking sheet, lightly oiled

a stove-top grill pan

Serves 4

Cut the tomatoes in half, spike with slivers of garlic, sprinkle with a little of the olive oil and arrange on a baking sheet. Roast in a preheated oven at 180°C (350°F) Gas 4 for about 1 hour, or until wilted and some of the moisture has evaporated.

Meanwhile, put the bread onto a preheated stove-top grill pan and cook until lightly toasted and charred with marks on both sides. Tear or cut the toast into pieces and put into a large salad bowl. Sprinkle with a little water until damp.

Add the tomatoes, cucumber, onion and parsley, then add salt and black pepper to taste. Sprinkle with the olive oil and vinegar, toss well, then set aside for about 1 hour to develop the flavours.

Add the fresh basil leaves and caperberries or capers and serve.

In Italian markets, you see boxes of different baby leaves. Shoppers choose a handful each of their favourite kinds to make a mixed salad. Originally, the mixture was picked from wild plants in the fields (*campo* means 'field') and still is in country areas, so the mixture should include herbs, bitter leaves, soft greens and crunchy leaves. In my supermarket, I find it best to choose a herb salad mixture, then add extra watercress, rocket and lamb's lettuce.

insalata di campo

350 g wild leaves or herbs

1 tablespoon balsamic vinegar

6–8 tablespoons extra virgin olive oil

freshly squeezed juice of ½ lemon

sea salt and freshly ground black pepper

50 g Parmesan cheese, in the piece, to serve

Serves 4–6

Wash the leaves well in a large bowl of cold water. Drain and shake or spin dry without crushing or bruising them. Transfer to a clean cloth lined with kitchen paper, wrap in the cloth and keep in the refrigerator for about 30 minutes.

Put the vinegar, oil and lemon juice into a small bowl, then add salt and black pepper to taste and beat well.

Using a swivel-bladed vegetable peeler, remove long, thin curls of Parmesan from the block, then set them aside.

When ready to serve, put the leaves into a large salad bowl. Whisk the dressing briefly and sprinkle over the salad. Toss gently until everything gleams, then top with the shavings of Parmesan and serve.

Note Choose a combination of leaves – whatever is fresh and good on the day. Suggestions include rocket, young dandelion leaves, lamb's lettuce, flat leaf parsley, baby spinach, sprigs of fresh dill and nasturtium leaves.

We have found that the peppers stuffed with melted goats' cheese are a particular favourite with guests, especially vegetarians – serve three halves with a few leaves of rocket as an easy, spectacular starter, even for a formal dinner, or this way as an accompaniment to main courses.

stuffed roasted peppers
with goats' cheese, pesto and roasted vegetables

500 g butternut squash or green-skinned pumpkin, cut into 3 cm wedges

2 sweet potatoes, cut into 3 cm chunks

2 red onions, quartered lengthways into wedges

125 ml extra virgin olive oil, plus extra for sprinkling

4 medium tomatoes, halved

sea salt flakes and freshly ground black pepper

Stuffed peppers

2 red and 2 yellow peppers, halved and deseeded

a handful of fresh basil leaves

8 cherry tomatoes, halved

8 teaspoons Classic Basil Pesto (page 71)

about 100 g mature goats' cheese, cut into 8 chunks

To serve

lemon wedges

ciabatta or focaccia bread, char-grilled

Serves 4–8

To make the stuffed peppers, brush a large roasting tin with olive oil and add the peppers, cut side up. Put a basil leaf, a halved cherry tomato, a spoonful of pesto and a chunk of goats' cheese into each pepper half.

Put the butternut squash or pumpkin, sweet potatoes and red onions into a plastic bag, add the 125 ml olive oil, salt and black pepper, then shake until everything is well coated in oil. Add them to the roasting tin, leaving space around each piece (use 2 roasting tins if necessary), then add the tomato halves. Sprinkle with salt, pepper and olive oil.

Put the tin or tins into a preheated oven at 200°C (400°F) Gas 6 or as high as your oven will go, and roast for about 30 minutes or until all the vegetables are tender and brown at the edges.

Serve with fresh basil leaves, lemon wedges and char-grilled ciabatta.

You can part-prepare the chickpeas, so the dressing soaks in well, then add the fresh ingredients just before serving. You can add any number of other ingredients, including olives, Parma ham, salami or chorizo, canned tuna, other vegetables, leaves or herbs, and a few of your favourite spices. Whatever takes your fancy in your Italian deli.

chickpea salad

1 kg cooked or canned chickpeas, rinsed and drained

250 g marinated artichoke hearts

250 g sun-blushed (semi-dried) tomatoes (optional)*

250 g very ripe cherry tomatoes, halved

8 spring onions, finely sliced diagonally

leaves from 8 sprigs of fresh basil, torn

a small bunch of fresh chives, scissor-snipped

leaves from 4 sprigs of fresh flat leaf parsley, chopped

50 g Parmesan cheese, shaved

1 tablespoon black pepper, cracked with a mortar and pestle

Dressing

6 tablespoons extra virgin olive oil

1 tablespoon freshly squeezed lemon juice
1 teaspoon Dijon mustard (optional)

1 small garlic clove, crushed

sea salt and freshly ground black pepper

Serves 4

Put all the dressing ingredients into a mixing bowl and beat with a fork or small whisk. Alternatively, put into a screw-top jar and shake well to form an emulsion.

Put the chickpeas, artichoke hearts and sun-blushed tomatoes, if using, into a bowl. Pour over the dressing. Cover with a lid and chill in the refrigerator for up to 4 hours.

When ready to serve, add the cherry tomatoes, spring onions, basil, chives and parsley. Stir gently, then sprinkle with shavings of Parmesan and black pepper.

*Note Sun-blushed tomatoes are partly dried sun-dried tomatoes.

italian dressings

vinaigrette

1 tablespoon white or red wine vinegar

5 tablespoons extra virgin olive oil

sea salt and freshly ground white pepper

Serves 4

Put all the ingredients into a mixing bowl or screw-top jar and beat or shake well to form an emulsion. If preferred, mix the dressing directly in the salad bowl, put the salad on top and leave undisturbed (no longer than 30 minutes), then toss just before serving.

extra virgin olive oil

Dispense with any acidity at all: simply pour superb, estate-bottled olive oil over the hot or warm food – grills, barbecued fish, warm vegetables, pasta. Even better, serve in small bowls with fresh crusty bread for dipping – heaven!

mayonnaise

2 egg yolks, at room temperature

2 teaspoons Dijon mustard

$1/4$ teaspoon salt

2 teaspoons fresh lemon juice or white wine vinegar

200 ml extra virgin olive oil

125 ml safflower oil or other light oil

Serves 4

Put the yolks into a medium bowl. Stir in the mustard, salt and half the lemon juice or vinegar and beat until smooth. Mix the oils in a measuring cup, then gradually pour the oil into the bowl, beating constantly to form a stiff, glossy emulsion. When all the oil has been added, taste, then beat in the remaining lemon juice or vinegar if necessary. Taste and adjust the seasoning.

Alternatively, to make in a blender or food processor, add 1 extra whole egg to the main recipe—the position of the blades means there is inadequate friction, so you need extra volume. This method works very well, though the emulsion is denser and less fluffy.

dolci

A superb basic Italian gelato recipe, made with cream rather than milk. It produces rather a large quantity, so divide the mixture into two or three parts, add a different flavouring to each, then churn separately.

gelato di crema

1 litre whipping cream or single cream

5 egg yolks

250 g caster sugar

Choice of flavourings

4 tablespoons liqueur, such as Italian Strega, Grand Marnier, sweet Marsala wine, dark or golden rum

fruit juices or purées, such as pineapple, passionfruit pulp, peach, mandarin, blackberry, raspberry

an ice cream machine or shallow freezer-proof boxes

Makes about 1.5 litres

Pour the cream into a small heavy-based saucepan and heat gently.

Put the egg yolks and sugar into a large bowl and, using an electric whisk or balloon whisk, beat until pale and creamy. Beat 2 tablespoons of the hot cream into the egg mixture to warm the yolks, then beat in the remaining cream, little by little.

Pour into the top of a double boiler, or into a heatproof bowl set over a saucepan of simmering water. Cook over gentle heat, stirring constantly, until the mixture is thick enough to coat the back of a wooden spoon. Do not let boil, or the mixture will curdle.

Let cool, then chill in the refrigerator until very cold. Transfer to an ice cream machine and churn*. Serve immediately or transfer to a freezer-proof container and freeze for later use.

If you don't have an ice cream machine, pour the mixture into shallow freezer-proof boxes and let part-freeze until ice crystals form around the edges. Remove from the freezer and beat with a fork or blender. Return to the freezer and part-freeze again. The more you freeze and beat, the smoother the ice cream will be.

Let soften in the refrigerator for about 20 minutes before serving.

*Note If you wish to add flavourings, add them just before churning.

Italian gelati are often made with milk, and so are denser than when made with cream. When made with cream only, or a mixture of cream and milk, as here, they are even more delicious. Both this recipe and the one on the previous page are wonderful just with vanilla, but you can add other flavours, such as finely chopped chocolate.

rich traditional
gelato

500 ml milk

2 vanilla pods or ¼ teaspoon vanilla extract (optional)

3–4 egg yolks

125 g sugar

250 ml double or whipping cream

an ice cream machine or shallow freezer-proof boxes

Makes about 1 litre

Put the milk and vanilla, if using, into a heavy-based saucepan and heat to just below boiling point. Remove from the heat and set aside to infuse for 15 minutes. Remove the vanilla pods, if using.

Put the egg yolks into a mixing bowl and, using an electric whisk or balloon whisk, beat until creamy. Whisk 2 tablespoons of the hot milk into the egg mixture, then beat in the remaining milk, a little at a time. Stir in the sugar, then transfer to the top of a double boiler or a heatproof bowl set over a saucepan of simmering water. Cook over gentle heat, stirring constantly, until the mixture is thick enough to coat the back of a wooden spoon. Do not let boil, or the mixture will curdle.

Remove from the heat and dip the saucepan into a bowl of cold water to stop the cooking process. Let cool completely, stir in the cream, then put into an ice cream machine and churn. Serve immediately or transfer to a freezer-proof container and freeze for later use.

If you don't have an ice cream machine, pour the mixture into shallow freezer-proof boxes and let part-freeze until ice crystals form around the edges. Remove from the freezer and beat with a fork or blender. Return to the freezer and part-freeze again. The more you freeze and beat, the smoother the ice cream will be.

Let soften in the refrigerator for 20 minutes before serving.

*Note If adding flavourings, add them just before churning.

Tiramisu is probably Italy's most popular pudding, beloved of those with a sweet tooth, wherever they live. It is the basis of this thoroughly wicked concoction. Sweet Marsala wine is the traditional flavouring, but rum could also be used.

gelato di tiramisu

8 sponge fingers

sweet Marsala wine or rum (see method)

250 ml mascarpone cheese

3–6 tablespoons strong espresso coffee, chilled

Zabaglione gelato

150 g sugar

3 egg yolks

250 ml double cream

4 tablespoons sweet Marsala wine

To decorate

whipped cream

shaved dark chocolate

an ice cream machine

2 freezer-proof boxes

Serves 6–8

To make the zabaglione gelato, put the sugar and 250 ml water into a small, heavy-based saucepan and cook over medium heat until the sugar has completely dissolved. Remove from the heat. Put the egg yolks into a bowl and, using an electric mixer or balloon whisk, beat until pale and creamy. Whisk 2 tablespoons of the hot syrup into the eggs to warm the yolks, then gradually whisk the egg mixture back into the syrup – the mixture will froth, like zabaglione. Using a spoon, fold in the cream and Marsala, then transfer to an ice cream machine and churn.* Remove the gelato from the machine and transfer to a plastic freezer-proof box. Freeze.

Put the Marsala or rum into a small bowl, then dip in the sponge fingers. Break or chop into pieces and put into the second box.

Put the mascarpone and 3 tablespoons of the coffee into a large bowl and mix well. Taste, then add more coffee, if preferred. Spoon over the top of the sponge fingers. Chill until ready to serve.

To serve, remove the gelato from the freezer and dip into warm water so it can be unmoulded. Transfer it to the top of the mascarpone mixture, pressing it down gently, then invert the whole mixture onto a serving plate. Cut into slices and decorate each slice with whipped cream and shaved chocolate.

*__Note__ If you don't have an ice cream machine, see page 129 for the freezing method.

This lemon sorbet is very sweet – so if you prefer yours more tart, reduce the quantity of sugar. Strain the mixture before churning if you like, but many people like the extra zip of the lemon zest. When grating the zest, for this or any other sorbet, make sure none of the white pith is included, or the sorbetto will be unpleasantly bitter. An egg white, beaten to a froth, is often stirred into sorbetti before freezing, to lighten the texture.

sorbetto al limone

250 g sugar, or to taste
grated zest of 2 lemons
500 ml freshly
squeezed lemon juice

an ice cream machine

Makes about 900 ml

Put 125 ml water, the sugar and lemon zest into a small, heavy-based saucepan and cook over medium heat, stirring constantly, until the sugar has completely dissolved.

Let cool, chill in the refrigerator, then add the lemon juice. Strain, then put into an ice cream machine and churn. Serve immediately or transfer to a freezer-proof container and freeze for later use. Let soften in the refrigerator for 15 minutes before serving.

Variations

Lime sorbetto Substitute the same quantity of lime juice and zest for the lemon, then proceed as in the main recipe.

Mandarin sorbetto Substitute 500 ml mandarin or tangerine juice for the freshly squeezed lemon juice. Use the grated zest of 2 mandarins instead of the lemons and proceed as in the main recipe.

Blood orange sorbetto Substitute 500 ml orange juice for the mandarin juice, preferably from red blood oranges, and the grated zest of 1 orange, and proceed as in the main recipe.

This is one of Italy's most famous puddings. Make it just before you want to serve it, and make sure you are organized before you start — provide a green salad for your guests while you work in the kitchen or there may be a riot while they wait!

zabaglione

5 egg yolks

1 egg

8 tablespoons caster sugar

8 tablespoons Marsala wine

8–12 amaretti biscuits or *Brutti ma buoni* (see below)

Serves 4–6

Brutti ma buoni

Ugly-but-good biscuits

600 g almond paste, coarsely grated

2 egg whites

50 g candied citron, finely chopped

50 g candied orange peel, finely chopped

50 g candied lemon peel, finely chopped

25 g unskinned almonds, chopped

25 g pine nuts

icing sugar, for dusting

a large baking sheet

Makes 32

Put the egg yolks, egg and sugar into a heatproof bowl set over a saucepan of barely simmering water and stir well. Using an electric whisk, balloon whisk or rotary beater, whisk the mixture until it becomes first a stable, light froth, then a thick mousse-like consistency, about 10–15 minutes. Add the Marsala, 1 tablespoon at a time, beating constantly. (Check the water level from time to time – it tends to evaporate. Do not overfill when you top it up – the bowl and water must never touch.)

Remove the saucepan and bowl from the heat and continue whisking until the froth will hold its shape and stay thick when the whisk is lifted out. Serve warm in tall goblets or pretty tumblers set on small plates, with biscuits for dipping.

Variation

To serve as a *Semifreddo de Zabaglione*, beat the warm zabaglione until cool, then fold gently into 300 ml cream, firmly whipped. Freeze without stirring. To churn in an ice cream machine, do not whip the cream before folding together. Churn until set, about 20 minutes.

Brutti ma buoni

Put the almond paste and egg whites into a mixing bowl and, using a wooden spoon, beat well. Add the peels and stir briefly. Chill for 30 minutes.

Dust your hands with icing sugar. Take 1 teaspoon of the dough and roll it in one hand, pushing in some nuts with the other. Arrange 5 cm apart on an ungreased baking sheet and bake in a preheated oven at 150°C (300°F) Gas 2 for 30 minutes until golden and firm. Remove from the oven and let cool on the baking sheet, then transfer to wire racks and let cool completely. Store in an airtight container. Serve dusted with icing sugar.

This Mediterranean cake comes from Sicily, where they use olive oil instead of butter to make cakes. It can be served as a pudding – with a scoop of citrus sorbet or gelato – or as a cake with an espresso and a glass of ice-cold water. It is also wonderful with a glass of Italian lemon liqueur – Limoncello from the Naples area, or Limuneddu di Sicilia.

lemon polenta cake

shredded or grated zest and juice of 1 lemon

shredded or grated zest and juice of 1 orange

185 ml extra virgin olive oil

215 g caster sugar

¼ teaspoon salt

3 medium eggs

200 g semolina

1 teaspoon baking powder

115 g ground almonds

1 teaspoon almond essence

1 teaspoon orange flower water

4 tablespoons Cointreau, Grand Marnier or Limuneddu di Sicilia liqueur

a springform cake tin, 23 cm diameter, lightly oiled and base-lined

Serves 8–12

Reserve a little of the shredded lemon and orange zest and put the remainder into a bowl with the orange and lemon juice, olive oil, sugar, salt and eggs. Using an electric mixer or balloon whisk, whisk until light and fluffy and doubled in volume.

Sift the semolina and baking powder into a second bowl and add the ground almonds. Stir the almond essence and orange flower water into the egg mixture. Pour all at once into the dry ingredients and fold together, but do not overmix. Spoon into the prepared tin and smooth the surface.

Bake towards the top of a preheated oven at 160°C (325°F) Gas 3 for about 40–45 minutes or until pale gold at the edges and firm in the centre. A skewer pushed into the middle of the cake should come out clean.

Remove from the oven and let cool in the tin for about 10 minutes. Sprinkle the liqueur and reserved shredded zest over the top. Push the cake out, still on its loose metal base, and let cool on a wire rack for another 10 minutes. Remove the base and paper. Serve in wedges, warm or cool, but not chilled.

A wonderful pick-me-up on a hot summer afternoon – and one that can be easily adapted to other ingredients, such as tomato juice, orange and raspberry juice, and so on. Even if you don't usually take sugar in your coffee, you will probably prefer it in this granita.

coffee granita

6 tablespoons freshly ground coffee

1 litre boiling water

sugar, to taste

To serve (optional)

6 tablespoons whipped cream

50 g shaved dark chocolate

an 8-cup cafetière

a shallow freezer-proof box

Serves 6

Put the coffee into the cafetière and pour over the boiling water. Let brew for 3 minutes, then press the plunger and pour into a heatproof bowl or jug and stir in sugar to taste—it should be sweeter than you would usually like. Let cool, then transfer to the freezer-proof box and freeze.

When the mixture is frozen but not rock-hard, remove from the freezer. Using a sturdy fork, crush and break the frozen coffee into icy shards. Spoon the frappé into large coffee cups or tall glasses. Serve immediately either plain or topped with whipped cream and shaved dark chocolate.

Variations

Put 100 ml chilled espresso coffee, 2 scoops vanilla ice cream and 100 ml milk into a blender and blend well. Add sugar to taste and pour into 2 tall glasses.

Substitute crushed pineapple, pear or apricot nectar, or orange and raspberry juice for the espresso coffee.

index

acknowledgements

Recipes

Silvana Franco
Tomato focaccia, Basic pizza dough, Roasted pepper pizza, Aubergine with bresaola, rocket and parmesan, Quattro stagioni, Topsy turvy cherry tomato pizza, Prosciutto, rosemary and goat's cheese pizza, Wafer potato pizza, Pizza marinara, Mushroom with basil, chilli and garlic, Homemade pasta, Classic basil pesto, Classic tomato sauce, White spaghetti, Pasta con le vongole, Pasta e fagioli, Classic lasagne.

Ursula Ferrigno
Saffron risotto, Risotto with asparagus, peas and basil, Artichoke risotto.

Clare Ferguson
Bagna cauda, Peperoni farciti, Black olives sott'olio, Green olives with fennel, Mussels with garlic, parsley and lemon, Clams with chilli parsley sauce, Focaccia with olives, Semolina gnocchi, Gnocchi with tomato sauce, Basic risotto, Sea bass parcels, Italian roast chicken, Polpetti al limone/meatballs with lemon, Osso buco, Char-grilled beef fillet, Italian risotto cake, The vinaigrette family, Insalata di campo, Zabaglione, Lemon polenta cake.

Elsa Petersen-Schepelern
Anchovy pastry pinwheels, Spice-speckled cheese straws, Mini pizzas, Grilled Italian antipasto, Tonno e fagioli, Insalata gonzaga, Italian pumpkin bean soup, Tuscan ribollita, Pumpkin soup, Italian mushroom soup, Fettuccine with pesto and gorgonzola sauce, Pumpkin risotto, Neapolitan seafood stew, Tuscan panzanella, Warm roasted vegetable salad, Chickpea salad, Gelato di crema, Rich traditional gelato, Gelato di tiramisu, Sorbetto al limone, Coffee granita.

Photography

Peter Cassidy
Pages 2–3, 4–5, 6–7, 17, 18, 21–23, 25, 26, 29, 30, 35, 39 above left, 70, 84, 88 below left, above left and right,100–101, 104, 107, 113–115,117, 118, 121, 122, 124, 138.

William Lingwood
Page 1, 8–11, 13, 14, 32–33, 36, 39 above right, below left and below right, 40, 42–43, 44–46, 49–51, 53, 54, 64, 73, 74, 79, 80, 83.

Jeremy Hopley
Pages 61, 67, 68 above left, below left and right, 77, 86, 91, 92, 99, 103, 108, 111, 137.

James Merrell
Pages 126–128, 131,132, 134, 141, 144.

Debi Treloar
Pages 58, 63 and endpapers.

Jason Lowe
Pages 56–57, 88 below right, 95, 96.

Recipes in this book were previously published in other Ryland Peters & Small cookbooks, including *Pizza* and *Pasta* by Silvana Franco; *Risotto* by Ursula Ferrigno; *Chicken: from Maryland to Kiev, Antipasti, Extra Virgin: Cooking with Olive Oil*, and *Flavours of Italy* by Clare Ferguson; *Fingerfood, Grill Pan Cooking, Salads, Pumpkin Butternut and Squash, Big Bowl, Blended Soups, Gelati Sorbets and Ice Creams*, and *Smoothies and Other Blended Drinks* by Elsa Petersen-Schepelern.